DAVID ROCCO'S DOLCE VITA

WWW.DAVIDROCCO.COM

DAVID ROCCO'S DOLCE VITA

Photography by
Francesco Lastrucci

Additional photography by
Devon Tsz-Kin Hong and Rutendo Sabeta

HarperCollinsPublishersLtd

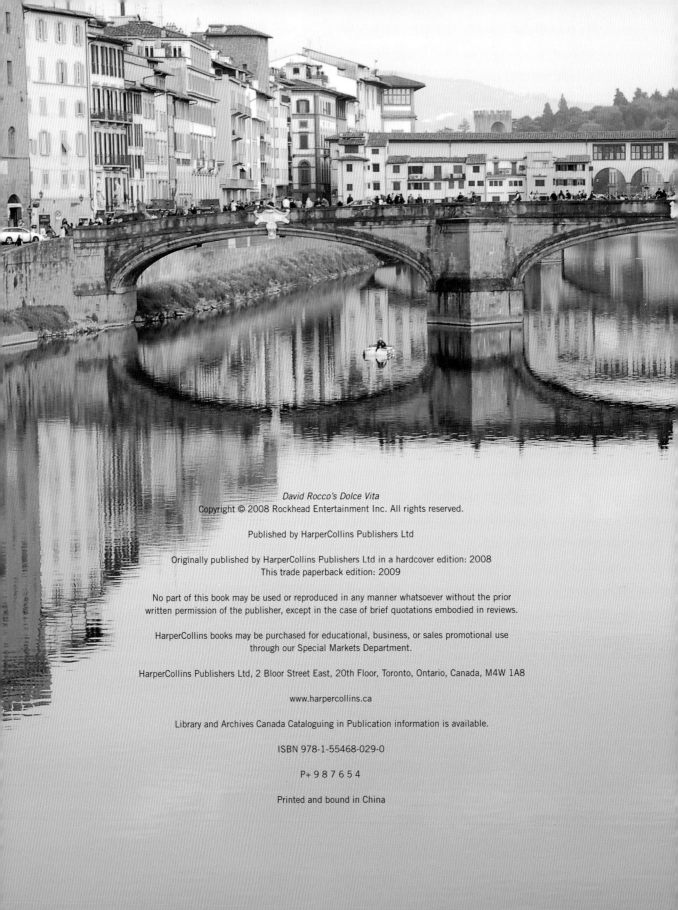

Published by HarperCollins Publishers Ltd

Originally published by HarperCollins Publishers Ltd in a hardcover edition: 2008
This trade paperback edition: 2009

HarperCollins books may be purchased for educational, business, or sales promotional use
through our Special Markets Department.

HarperCollins Publishers Ltd, 2 Bloor Street East, 20th Floor, Toronto, Ontario, Canada, M4W 1A8

www.harpercollins.ca

Library and Archives Canada Cataloguing in Publication information is available.

ISBN 978-1-55468-029-0

P+ 9 8 7 6 5 4

Printed and bound in China

To my beautiful wife, Nina,

my partner, my inspiration and my love.

You are my dolce vita!

Contents

QUANTO BASTA

When I was a kid, my parents used to take my brother, my sister and me to Italy during summer vacation. I loved the food, so no matter what was going on, I inevitably ended up hanging out with the *nonne*, the grandmothers, in their kitchens. What they did with a few ingredients struck me as magic, as alchemy. Even at that young age, I was aware of the importance of food and its power to bring people together, to nourish more than the stomach. Watching them work with ease and good humor in their simple kitchens, making food in the traditional ways handed down over generations, I felt that cooking was part of their DNA. I also felt it was part of mine. But the thing I really loved was that when I'd ask how much of a certain ingredient to add, they'd always say, "*Quanto basta*," which roughly translates as "As much as you need" or "As much as you like."

As time has gone on, I've come to see that *quanto basta*, or QB, is more than a recipe instruction. It's a bit of folk wisdom that can guide you in life. What it says is to take as much as you need and no more. Moderation and balance.

Quanto basta is a philosophy that should empower you to embrace inspiration and inventiveness through the alchemy of cooking, knowing that this magical transformation will happen if you let it. When you stop worrying about the outcome, you'll be swept away by the magic in the food and the process. And allowing that will give you joy and feed your soul.

My hope is that this book inspires you to find freedom and confidence—both in the kitchen and in your life.

DOLCE VITA

Literally translated, *dolce vita* means "sweet life." Life has its ups and downs, but I believe you can find a little *dolce vita* even on the worst days.

To me, *dolce vita* has nothing to do with money or social status or possessions. It's about being present in those moments in life that bring you joy. It's a sip of perfect espresso in the morning. It's the patina of a rugged old kitchen table that has seen a thousand family dinners. It's a nod hello to a stranger as you struggle down the street in the morning to catch the bus.

Dolce vita is linked to food, cooking and family. I remember waking up on Sunday mornings and hearing my mom in the kitchen, with the radio tuned to an Italian station. Then would come our weekly dance. I'd sneak into the kitchen, and she'd pretend not to notice as I ripped a piece of bread from the fresh loaf on the counter and dipped it into the tomato sauce gently bubbling away on the stove, richly flavored by meat that would later become two courses of our Sunday *pranzo*. Then I'd head to the den and sit down with my dad to watch some soccer. The air would be rich with the smell of his espresso, and I'd get a little poured into my glass of warm milk. There's no perfume that smells as sweet to me as Sunday morning in the Rocco household.

Those early memories of food and family are intertwined in the Italian psyche. Years later, I remember taking a drive down the Amalfi coast with my wife, Nina, and a few of our friends, arguing the whole time about whose mamma made the best melanzane alla parmigiana or lasagna. I can't tell you how many times I've had those kinds of conversations with Italian friends. The supremacy of mamma's cooking is a point of pride for most Italians.

That's *dolce vita*!

SIMPLICITY

In Italy, there's a respect for and a connection to food that has come down through the generations. People eat together, sharing meals that often include several courses—antipasti, primi, secondi, contorni, dolci. But you'll rarely find anything on an Italian menu that's complex. For me, this simplicity is the heart of *dolce vita*.

There are very few fancy or heavy sauces in Italian cooking. The goal is to use the best ingredients you can get your hands on and to enhance their flavors, doing the very minimum. You don't need to worry about learning complex techniques or investing in fancy kitchen equipment to bring everything together.

A lot of the recipes that are prized in Italy have their roots in what's called *cucina povera*. It's cooking that originated with the farming class, people who lived simply off their land, eating seasonally because they had only what they harvested or what they could find locally. Nothing was allowed to go to waste, not even a tough crust of bread.

All over Italy, you'll run into festivals that celebrate the new crop of whatever native fruit or vegetable has just come into season. That respect for food shows itself in the way the ingredient is prepared—simply, so you get the full blast of freshness.

SENSUALITY

Eating is sensual. Preparing food can be just as sensual. Run your hands through a bag of beans. Mix ingredients for dough on a flat board. Get your hands in there and really connect with your food. I say this and believe it with all my heart: food responds to the attention you put into a meal. The more love you put into it, the better it tastes—and a good bottle of olive oil doesn't hurt either! I've had the experience of cooking when I was distracted, and the food just didn't taste the same. On the other hand, I've also had the experience of making a very humble, simple meal, but by really staying in the moment, appreciating the ingredients and paying attention to the process, the food ended up being extraordinary. Why does your grandmother's food always taste best? It's the love she puts into it.

ALCHEMY

Attention to the process is part of the alchemy of cooking. So is trusting that something magical is at work. Want proof? Boil some water and throw in some pasta. While that's cooking, grab your olive oil and pour some into the bottom of your heated frying pan. Then add some finely chopped garlic, a handful of fresh ripe cherry tomatoes that you've cut into quarters and let them all sauté gently in the olive oil. When that gets to a consistency that looks good to you, rip up a few basil leaves and toss them in.

Drain your pasta and add it to your cherry tomato sauce in the pan and mix it together. Now watch the transformation: the pasta will release its starches and thicken up the sauce, while the tomato sauce begins to stick to the pasta. Maybe finish it by grating a little bit of your favorite cheese on top and drizzling some of your best olive oil over the whole thing. Now taste it. Suddenly, from water and flour and simple cherry tomatoes, you've made a dish that's out of this world. You've created alchemy using the most ordinary ingredients.

And I think there's a parallel here for one's life: even the simplest rituals or moments can be *dolce vita*.

BALANCE

There's a balance and a simplicity to cooking that can be reflected in one's life. Get away from the clutter. Simplify. The more stuff we have, the more confusion we have around us, and the more we feel overwhelmed. We can work more hours, but that never seems to translate into more satisfaction. It comes back to *quanto basta*. It's not about being excessive; it's about respecting the food, the ingredients. Just because a sprinkle of really good Parmigiano tastes great doesn't mean you add more. Too much—even of a good thing—does not make it better. It's about making a choice to use only what you need, and nothing more.

CONNECTION

When Nina and I lived in Rome, we knew very few people, so we used food to create a connection with others. Whether it was getting to know the market vendors in Campo dei Fiori or inviting new friends over for a simple meal, food broke down barriers fast and brought people together. When you open your home to friends and family, you'll be amazed at how the alchemy in your kitchen can become the alchemy that changes your life. Breaking bread with people is magical. Food unites and connects us all.

WHAT YOU NEED TO KNOW

My biggest hope is that you use this book to inspire you. If you've never cooked or are a bit nervous in the kitchen, then you may want to follow the recipes as written the first few times. If you're more confident, then I urge you to follow your instincts and adapt them to your taste. Below are some important considerations to keep in mind when reading the recipes.

The seasonings, especially for salt and pepper, are given as QB (*quanto basta*), which, as Italian cooks know, means "to your own taste."

I use cold-pressed extra-virgin olive oil for everything, from frying to finishing off my salads. So when I say olive oil in a recipe, I always mean extra-virgin. It's one of the healthiest and most digestible oils out there, especially in its purest raw state. There have been times when my wife, Nina, and I have gone to a dinner party with a bottle of fresh olive oil for the hosts instead of a bottle of wine.

Even among cold-pressed extra-virgin olive oils, there are variations. Some are fruitier, some grassier. Some are blends that are meant to be more neutral. Experiment to find the ones you like. I generally have two on hand: a good-quality oil that I use for cooking and frying, and the second oil, the best I can find, for dressing salads or drizzling over finished meat or pasta dishes. Just a little light touch can completely elevate a dish. Believe me, there's a difference between french fries made in olive oil and fries done in regular vegetable oil, or worse. Of course, you can alter the amount to suit your taste and your diet.

In Italy, a good olive oil bottle has a best-before date because, ideally, it should be consumed within a year to a year and a half of being pressed. In general, once you've opened a bottle, store it away from the light, in a dry, cool place.

When you're frying, make sure your olive oil is hot before you add your ingredients; you want to crisp the food quickly so it won't absorb the oil and become too heavy. I've never used a thermometer, and never known anyone who has. To test the temperature of oil, I throw in a tiny bit of bread or, if I'm using a batter, a bit of the beaten egg. If it sizzles, you're good to go. You'll know your oil is too hot if it starts smoking; just turn the heat down.

A note about herbs: use fresh. In fact, if you have any dried herbs in your cupboard, put this book down right now and throw them out! Okay, so maybe I'm overreacting, but just slightly. Basil, parsley, coriander, thyme, rosemary and oregano add beautiful fresh flavor. You won't even get close to the same effect with dried, and especially not from those old bottles that have been languishing in the back of your cupboard. Fresh herbs have a special fragrance that brings a unique sweet, earthy taste to your dishes. There are exceptions. For instance, a pizzaiola sauce is traditionally made with dried oregano. But I still prefer making my pizzaiola sauce with fresh. To me, it's better.

Which brings me to the most important instruction of all: taste. Taste as you go, because that's the only way you'll know whether the dish is turning out to your liking. It's important that you season a bit at a time. You can't take salt out of a dish, so rather than overdo it, go easy. I don't know any great cooks or chefs who don't taste.

There's a visual component to cooking as well. For instance, when you're making a sauce, you'll be able to judge how much longer you need to cook it by how it looks. This may take some practice, but by watching the transformation during the cooking process, you'll come to know intuitively when something is done, based on what you see.

It's the same when you're following a recipe. If the recipe calls for a cup of something but half a cup looks good to you, go with your instincts and your own taste.

Don't be afraid to mess up. These recipes are, for the most part, forgiving. As well, you're using good basic ingredients, so even if the recipe is slightly off, the integrity of the ingredients will pull you through. Besides, I don't know a cook or chef, no matter how experienced, who doesn't have the occasional mishap. Sometimes those mishaps are tasty!

Then there's the issue of ingredients. Just because you don't have one of the smaller ingredients at hand, don't let that discourage you from making a recipe. For instance, some recipes call for wine. If you don't have any wine, you can use a little brandy. If you don't use alcohol, replace it with water. I've had great results making risotto with water when I didn't have any stock or wine on hand.

Generally, the recipes don't tell you whether or not to use a lid. I leave that to you. Most of the time, I cook without a lid because I like to watch the dish evolve. Of course, if I'm cooking something that has to simmer for a long time, the lid goes on.

Ingredients vary from city to city, country to country, season to season. Cooking times can vary depending on whether you use a gas or electric stove. Also, the quality of your pots and pans can affect heat transfer and therefore cooking time. Some pots get hot more quickly; cooking with them on high heat will scorch everything. Others take a longer time and work best on higher heat. The same goes for ovens: some are hotter than others even when they're turned to the same temperature. So use this book as a guide, not a bible.

GOOD INGREDIENTS

Simple, Seasonal, Fresh

I think the *fortuna* of the Italians is that they live on a rich peninsula with fertile soil under the Mediterranean sun. But more important, Italians respect what they have. They've never lost their connection to the land and to their food. They've never allowed fast farming methods to replace the age-old traditional ways that give them some of the best ingredients in the world, from the pomodorini to wine to olive oil.

And this is key: good Italian cuisine is all about simple, seasonal, fresh ingredients, simply prepared. In fact, some of the best of Italian cooking is more about assembly. You'll hear me say that again and again throughout this book.

In North America, we're brought up believing that you should be able to have any food you want all year round. We've lost the appreciation for the seasonality of food. Many of my friends in Italy look forward to the seasons and associate them with the arrival of certain produce. Spring is asparagus. Late summer brings figs and peaches. And fall means truffles and chestnuts. All over Italy, there are *sagre,* or food festivals, to celebrate particular local ingredients when they come into season.

There's also a consciousness about how to use what nature has given you. So it doesn't necessarily follow that if something is good then more of it has to be better. Not only is it not better, but in some cases it can completely disrupt the simplicity of another ingredient. It's really about respecting the truth of each ingredient and how each can accompany and complement the other and come into true harmony.

Canned, Frozen or Dried

There are times when it's completely permissible to use canned or frozen vegetables. Tomatoes are in season for a short time. The canned variety are picked and packed at their peak. Buy canned tomatoes with no added ingredients, and that means no salt, sugar or basil. Frozen vegetables are also picked at their peak and therefore acceptable substitutes for fresh. Italians, especially Tuscans, use a lot of legumes. Cooking them from scratch is simple but time-consuming, so I always have cans of my favorite beans and lentils in the cupboard. Just make sure you drain and rinse them before using. If you want to cook dried ones from scratch, cover them with water, soak them overnight and drain. Cover them with fresh water and bring to a boil, then simmer for about 40 minutes or until tender. If you go this route, make a little extra. Once they've cooled, put them in freezer bags and freeze them. They'll hold for months.

Stock

Some recipes call for stock. You'll find basic chicken, meat, fish, and vegetable stock recipes in the Zuppe section. They're easy to make and add wonderful flavor. But don't let a lack of stock prevent you from making a particular recipe. Unless cooking is your full-time job, you may not have the time to make your own. While a good homemade stock will give your dish depth of flavor, it's fine to use just plain old water. No matter what, though, do *not* use a bouillon cube or powdered soup flavor enhancer. Many of them are full of fat, and high in sodium, MSG and other chemicals that aren't good for you. Besides, it's just not necessary. Even for a risotto, I would rather add a little more wine and an extra sprinkle of Parmigiano-Reggiano for flavor.

KITCHEN ESSENTIALS

I'm not big on kitchen gadgets or tools. First-time guests at our house are always shocked to find that I don't even have a food processor. Food just doesn't taste as good to me unless it's chopped by hand. And, quite frankly, I know a lot of Italian *nonne* who can cook as well as any top chef at a five-star restaurant, and they do it in their three- by three-foot apartment kitchens without any fancy appliances!

A food processor may be efficient, but it takes away the sensual part of cooking—touching and handling your food. You can read all the cookbooks in the world or watch all the cooking shows on television, but nothing will help you develop your sense of smell, your ability to eyeball your ingredients or your understanding of how an ingredient functions better than doing it all by hand.

If I'm making a dish that requires dough, I'd rather touch it with my hands. I like to rip my basil. But if something calls for finely chopped basil, I'll get out my wooden cutting board and a mezzaluna or chef's knife and go for it. That way, I don't bruise the herbs, and the payoff is the release of their perfumes. Even a simple pesto can be made on a cutting board (see page 175).

You can create a pesto in the time it takes to cook your pasta. Even if it's not perfect, it's going to give your dish character. You'll see this transformation happen right in front of you, and intuitively you'll start to understand. And think about how much better it will taste after you've connected with it.

Okay, now that I've convinced you to go "hand-held," here's what's in my kitchen. I'm strictly low-tech: I have a mezzaluna, a great set of knives and, when I need to purée, an immersion blender that goes right into the pot. I love a large, heavy cutting board, something that doesn't warp and is big enough that you can multitask on it. And I have a great set of pots and pans. *Basta!*

Il Mercato

The Italian market is an incredible place. It's not just about food; it's about community. There's a rhythm to market life. The rhythm is also connected to the seasons. Italians are not removed from the food they eat. And from season to season, and week to week within the season, they head to the market to buy the best and freshest of the local crops.

The market is also a bit of theater in the daily routine. There are the local characters who hang out there. The vendors themselves are often characters. The whole scene can be very animated, boisterous, a bit crazy at times and a lot of fun. And there's a sensuality to the markets as well, with the newest offerings of the season piled up in a riot of colors and textures. There's also a bit of flirting that goes on between clients and vendors, part of the whole dance of daily life.

The artisanal tradition has never needed to be revived in Italy because it never ceased. In the Italian marketplace, you'll find yourself coaxed over to the cheese-monger's stall, where he'll cut you a piece of his latest cheese, not because he wants to make a sale but because he's proud of what he has. Or he may want your opinion on a new cheese he's sourced and brought to market. More often than not, it's the guy who was milking the sheep who is selling the ricotta salata, not someone who was kicked out of the house and told by his mother to get a part-time job!

At the market, shoppers will go to the same vendors daily, and that's both a pleasurable game and a measure of loyalty. The first time you encounter a vendor, she might be cranky or standoffish, but if you like what she's selling and keep going, pretty soon that cranky vendor will be waiting for you with suggestions based on what she knows you like. Don't be surprised when you show up to find she's tucked away something special for your daily visit. And it's not unusual for a vendor to offer you recipes for using the new produce of the season. The vendors are foodies themselves. They get excited about what's new and are anxious to pass it on. If you buy vegetables, they'll throw in an herb bundle to use when you cook them. The next day, they'll want to know how you liked it, and so it goes. This extends your community to include one more person.

Another thing you'll notice at an Italian market is that the fruits and vegetables don't look perfect. In North America, you'll find stacks of perfect-looking produce: shiny red apples, waxed to make them look flawless; oranges that are uniformly orange and round. Everything's so perfect it looks fake! But at a market in Italy, you won't find that. The apples don't look perfect because they're truly organic. There's no homogeneous view of what an apple *should* look like. Rather, there's an understanding that what's important is how it tastes.

Another important thing you're doing when you go to the market is supporting the family-owned farm or business. The producers are the true pillars of the food industry. It's their passion, their love for what they do and the devotion to their products that make the ingredients amazing. It's not a faceless mega-corporation. You know where the food comes from.

INSALATA DEL MERCATO BALLARÒ
Ballarò Market Salad

This salad was inspired by Palermo's Mercato Ballarò. Even for Italians, who shop at markets on a daily basis, the Palermo markets are a must-see, a true pulse of the city. The three major markets are among the oldest in Europe. They're vibrantly gritty, chaotic places, with vendors lined up on either side of the narrow streets shouting out their daily specials like stage actors, creating their own kind of street theater. In the heart of these markets, the fruit and vegetable vendors put out baskets of colorful produce and, next to them, pots of freshly boiled or grilled vegetables for the Palermitani as they do their daily shopping. Don't be fooled by the simplicity of these ingredients. Like the markets, this rustic salad has real character.   **PER 4 PERSONE**

2 sweet yellow peppers
2 onions
2 large potatoes, peeled
1/2 lb (250 g) string beans, trimmed
Extra-virgin olive oil, QB
Salt and freshly ground pepper, QB

Roast the peppers by following Zia Franca's method (see page 48) or by broiling them in the oven for about 30 minutes, turning every so often until the skin is charred. Remove them and put them in a paper bag to allow the steam to lift the skin. Or put them in a bowl and cover with a dishtowel. When they've cooled down, peel off the skin, remove the seeds and slice them.

Remove the papery outer layer from the onions. Place the whole onions on a baking sheet and roast in a 400°F (200°C) oven until they've softened and lost their shape, and are golden and caramelized. It will take about 1 hour, but check after half an hour. Let cool until you can handle them. Slice.

In separate pots, boil the potatoes and string beans in salted water until soft. When they're cool enough to handle, cube the potatoes. Now put the potatoes, string beans, onions and peppers together in a nice serving bowl. Add extra-virgin olive oil, salt and pepper, and enjoy!

You can roast the peppers and onions a day ahead. Just let them cool before you store them in the fridge.

Un' altra idea: If you have leftovers, get a great bun, slice up some pecorino cheese and add some of this salad. It will knock your socks off.

Antipasti, Sfizi e Contorni

I love this chapter! The theory in Italian cooking is that you serve dishes in a specific order to achieve a certain kind of eating experience. Traditionally, antipasti are little bites to nibble on before the meal starts. When I'm making a multi-course meal, I use antipasti to help set the tone of the evening and to pace the meal. The sides, or contorni, are what accompany the main dish. They're usually vegetables done simply but beautifully. Which brings me to sfizi. Sfiziosi are fun foods, nibbles—the kind of little bite you'd serve with cocktails. But they're so simple and so delicious that you can make them any time you want.

There's nothing stopping you from making antipasti, contorni or sfizi your meal. Sometimes when I go to a restaurant, I order a bunch of sides, along with a bottle of wine and some great bread, and that's my meal. Or when I'm entertaining at home, I occasionally borrow from the Spanish and serve a selection of dishes, tapas style. It's more informal and social.

ANTIPASTO DI RICOTTA
Simple Ricotta Antipasto

Ricotta is such a versatile cheese. It can be used in every course, from antipasti to dessert. In Italy, the taste of ricotta and the specialties made with it vary slightly in different parts of the country. Cows or sheep that graze in the north eat grass and drink water that's different from the grass and water in the south, and live in a different climate. Such factors give ricotta a distinctive taste from region to region, and even season to season. In Sicily, many *pasticcerie* will tell you that their cannoli taste best in the winter and early spring because the grass that the sheep graze on during those seasons makes the cheese a little bit more flavorful. Sheep's milk ricotta is sharper than the version made with cow's cheese. I recommend using it for this recipe because it gives this dish more flavor. If you can't find it, cow's milk ricotta will do.

Sheep's milk ricotta, freshly ground pepper, lemon zest, extra-virgin olive oil

There's no real science to preparing this dish. This is how I do it. I put my ricotta in a big bowl and work it with a fork until creamy. Then I add a couple of grinds of pepper and mix to combine. Then it goes into a serving dish. I top it off with some lemon zest and a drizzle of olive oil. This is the time to break out your best extra-virgin. Serve this in the middle of the table, alongside some great fresh bread, and let your guests help themselves. It works really well with fresh figs and prosciutto.

Un' altra idea: Try a dessert version of this recipe. Mix ricotta cheese with some sugar, finely chopped semisweet chocolate and cocoa powder.

BRESAOLA

Pork has its prosciutto, and beef has bresaola. This is an Italian cured beef, sliced paper thin so that the pieces are almost transparent. First, the beef is seasoned with a dry rub of spices and coarse salt, and hung to dry for a few days. That's followed by a curing process of one to three months. The result is tender and full of flavor. Bresaola is usually served at room temperature or slightly chilled as part of an antipasto. The next two recipes are a couple of my favorite ways to enjoy it.

INVOLTINI DI BRESAOLA

When I serve this as an antipasto, I sometimes finish with a light drizzle of extra-virgin olive oil. For an antipasto for four, get about 16 slices of bresaola and about 1/2 lb (250 g) fresh sheep's ricotta. Mix the ricotta with a couple of tablespoons (30 mL) of good extra-virgin olive oil and some freshly ground pepper. Get yourself a bunch of fresh arugula and wash it and spin it dry. Lay a slice of bresaola on your work surface, drop a large spoonful of the ricotta mixture in the center, add a few arugula leaves and roll the whole thing up.

CARPACCIO DI BRESAOLA

I sometimes use bresaola as my "instant carpaccio." Talk about easy, and yet there's something almost elegant about this antipasto. Lay slices of bresaola on a serving platter. Cover them with arugula. Sprinkle with salt and freshly squeezed lemon juice. With a vegetable peeler, shave large pieces of Parmigiano-Reggiano cheese over top, then drizzle the whole thing with the best extra-virgin olive oil you have.

PEPPERONI DI ZIA FRANCA
Roasted Peppers Zia Franca Style

Expect this to be your new favorite dish for the next month. The good news is, the longer it sits, the better it gets. After tasting it, you'll want my Zia Franca's phone number so you can thank her. It's brilliant.

There are many ways to roast peppers: on the barbecue, on a baking tray in the oven or, as Zia Franca does, right on the open flame of a gas stovetop. The trick to roasting a pepper is to make sure you char it on all sides. You actually want the skin to look burnt. Don't panic! You're burning the skin, not the pepper. It will give the meat of the pepper a slightly smoky taste.

Once the peppers are fully roasted, put them in a paper bag and let them hang out. This gives them a steam bath and lifts the skin, making them easier to peel. Take them out of the bag and remove and discard the skin and seeds. You can run them under water to clean off any stubborn bits of charred skin and seeds. At this point, they're ready to use in your recipe. Or, if they're in season and you're making lots, put them into freezer bags. They hold well, and in the middle of winter you'll have freshly roasted peppers available in minutes.   **PER 4 PERSONE**

3 tbsp (45 mL) extra-virgin olive oil
2 cloves garlic, finely chopped
1 cup (250 mL) walnut halves
1/2 cup (125 mL) black olives, pitted
1/4 cup (50 mL) capers, drained
2 anchovies, finely chopped (optional)
2 roasted red peppers, sliced into strips
1/2 cup (125 mL) dry bread crumbs
1 bunch fresh flat-leaf parsley, chopped

In a saucepan, heat up the olive oil over high heat. Throw in the garlic. Keep an eye on it, and when it gets slightly brown, toss in your walnut halves, olives, capers and anchovies. The anchovies are optional; I've made this dish with and without them. If you're using them, chop them finely. They'll melt into the oil and give the dish loads of flavor.

After a minute or so, lower the heat to medium, add the roasted peppers, and cook for about 5 minutes, stirring every so often. Turn off the heat and set the pan aside. Sprinkle in the bread crumbs and parsley and mix to combine. Let cool. Serve at room temperature.

Il Forno

Even though supermarkets have made inroads into Italian food culture, I doubt that *il forno* will ever become extinct. Bread shops are one of Italy's most enduring and unique cultural experiences.

At your local *forno*, you're not obliged to buy an entire loaf; you buy only as much as you need. You go in, and it's *quanto basta*. You hold up your hands to show the baker the size of the portion you want, he cuts it and weighs it to figure out the price, and off you go. Like the market, it's more than just a place to get your food. It's a daily ritual, a little social event.

Italians' respect for bread is such that there's no throwing out leftovers. It's the philosophy of *l'arte di arrangiarsi*, "the art of making do." The ingenious Italian cuisine offers plenty of ways to use up stale bread that take advantage of its age. *Cucina povera*, or "peasant cuisine," which is now arguably the best and healthiest cuisine, is based on not letting anything go to waste. "*Non si butta nulla!*" It's disrespectful. And as alchemists in the kitchen, we can reinvent and make a virtue out of yesterday's bread. So that stale leftover becomes pappa al pomodoro or panzanella.

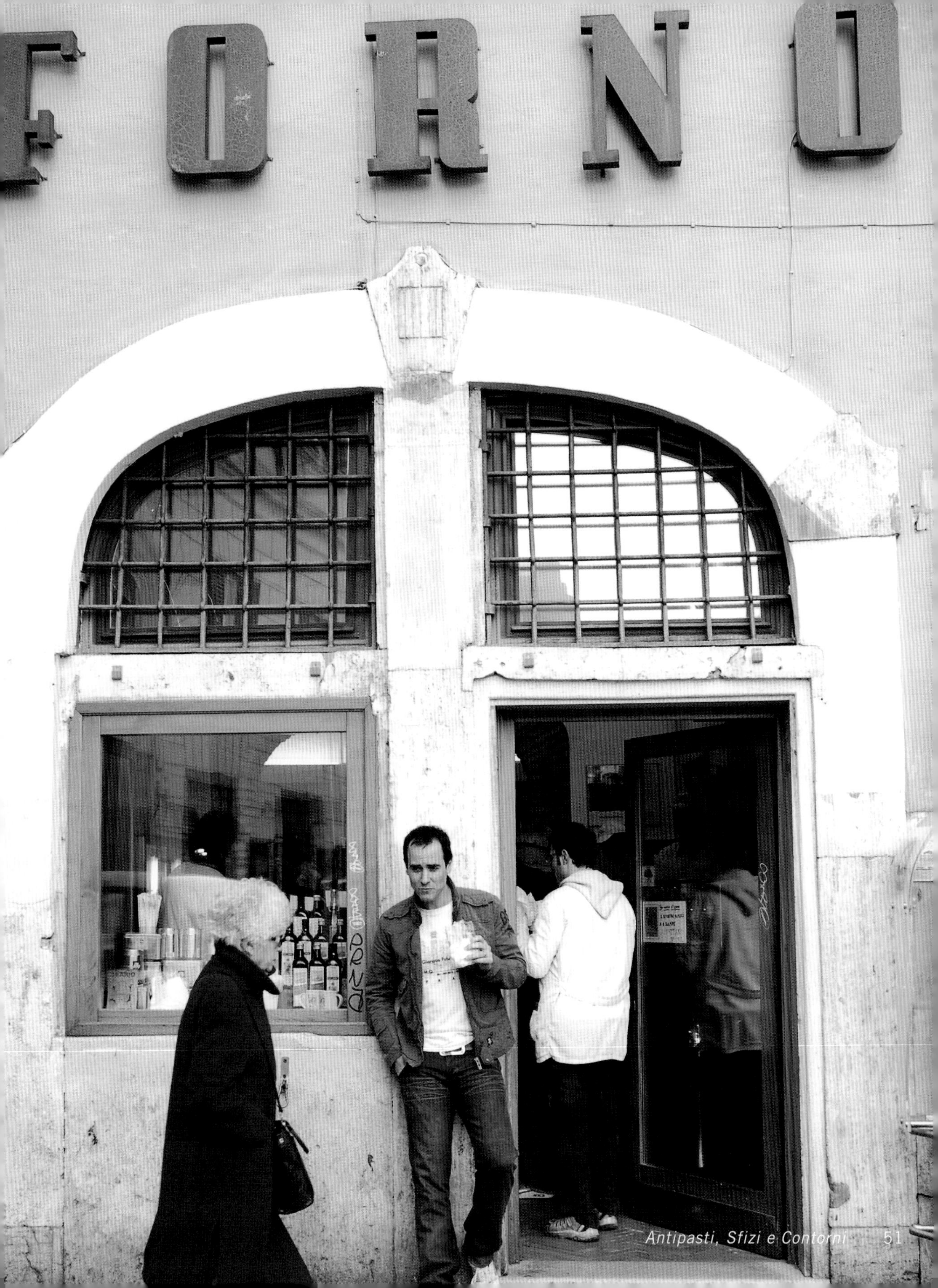
FORNO

PANE, BURRO E ZUCCHERO
Bread, Butter and Sugar

This snack is something Italian mammas make for their kids all the time. I know it sounds ridiculous, but try it—you'll absolutely love it! Spread some butter on bread slices and add a sprinkle of brown sugar. That's all there is to it—bread, butter, brown sugar. How can you go wrong?

PANE, ZUCCHERO E VINO
Bread, Sugar and Wine

This next snack is something every Italian mamma makes for her own pleasure! Sprinkle a bit of sugar on a slice of bread. Drizzle with a drop or two of wine and enjoy! Or you can do as my grandmother did: Dip the bread into a glass of wine, then sprinkle the wine-soaked bread with some sugar.

PANZANELLA
Tuscan Bread Salad

Panzanella represents the very essence of Tuscan cooking, the powerful ability to transform simple, poor ingredients—or worse, stale bread—into a brilliant meal.

As with most traditional recipes, there are many different spins. Some call for using cut tomatoes with the seeds and juices; some remove the seeds. Others suggest discarding the crust and toasting the bread. This is putting a *nouvelle* spin on it that I don't really agree with. This dish was created to make use of stale bread, not to take fresh bread and toast it! The soul of this recipe is in the transformation of the old bread and, to me, to do it any other way is nuts. I would also suggest making this dish in the height of summer, when you can use tomatoes fresh off the vine. Some ripped-up basil, some fantastic olive oil—I can taste it now. Here's my favorite way to make panzanella. It's simple, and it works for me every time. **PER 4 PERSONE**

8 slices stale Tuscan-style or dense country-style bread
10 cherry tomatoes, halved
1 red onion, thinly sliced
1/2 cup (125 mL) best-quality extra-virgin olive oil
2 tbsp (30 mL) red wine vinegar
4 fresh basil leaves
Salt and freshly ground pepper, QB

Submerge the slices of stale bread in a bowl of water. Get your hands in there and play with your food. You want to mush it around for a minute or so. Panzanella is all about texture, so by using your hands, you can decide how mushy you want it to be and how moist you want your final result to be. The food will respond to your touch and will taste better. Once you're done, squeeze out the water and break up the bread into your serving bowl.

If you're making this in peak season, when the tomatoes are sweet, then use the juice, seeds and all. Otherwise, squeeze the water and seeds out of your halved cherry tomatoes; discard the seeds. Add the tomatoes and sliced red onions to the bowl. Add the olive oil and red wine vinegar. Tear up the basil and add it along with salt and pepper.

Give it a good toss and let it rest in the fridge for 30 minutes to give the flavors a chance to develop before serving.

Un' altra idea: Add radicchio or arugula for some bite and a bit of crunch and color. Add just before serving so the greens don't wilt in the salad.

PAPPA AL POMODORO
Tomato and Stale Bread Soup

Talk about simple! Talk about true alchemy! This is a rustic Tuscan dish, and yet there's something so sensual about it. Until you've experienced it and have had it with some freshly pressed olive oil, you can't imagine how great it is. It has a wonderful intense, sweet, silky tomato taste. It makes my mouth water just to write about it. And it's one of those dishes that will taste even better if you wait half an hour after making it and let it cool down to room temperature.

The texture of this dish is soft and delicate, almost like baby food. In fact, the name *pappa al pomodoro* translates as "baby food with tomatoes," which is more about the texture than its target audience.

This dish is made during the olive harvest to take advantage of the brilliant flavor of the freshest Tuscan olive oil. Use the best you can find for this recipe. It calls for more oil than you might expect, but trust me—go with it.

PER 6 PERSONE

1 cup (250 mL) extra-virgin olive oil
2 stalks celery, finely chopped
2 carrots, finely chopped
1 onion, finely chopped
1 loaf stale Tuscan-style or dense country-style bread, cut into small pieces
2 cups (500 mL) vegetable stock
Salt and freshly ground pepper, QB
2 lb (1 kg) peeled fresh or canned plum tomatoes, with juices
5 fresh basil leaves

Start by making a soffritto (see page 153), heating 2/3 cup (150 mL) of the oil in a large pot over medium-high heat and sautéing the celery, carrots and onions slowly until soft and golden. Add the bread. Because the pot is hot, your bread might stick, so keep stirring. Make sure the bread pieces are fully coated with that great extra-virgin olive oil. Add a few ladles of vegetable stock and stir. Now you're on your way to creating the pappa. While you're stirring, the bread will break down and mix with the vegetables, becoming a nice soft pappa. Season with salt and pepper as you go. Remember that Tuscan bread is generally unsalted, so you'll likely have to add a little salt.

Add the plum tomatoes and break them up with the back of a wooden spoon. At this point, the texture will be mushy, like baby food. If the pappa is too dense and you prefer it soupier, just add more stock. Cook it over medium heat for 30 minutes. Let it cool down and rest a little bit, then finish it with a good drizzle of the remaining extra-virgin olive oil and some torn-up basil.

FETTUNTA
Tuscan "Bruschetta"

Fettunta means "wet sliced bread." During the olive harvest season, the Tuscans take fettunta literally and dunk entire pieces of bread in the freshly pressed barrels of extra-virgin olive oil. It's a tradition, and it's a must. It's also delicious, so if you have the good fortune to be in Tuscany during the harvest season, try it.

During the rest of the year, fettunta is scaled back a bit in terms of the amount of oil that's used. It becomes what many people would consider a simple bruschetta. Bruschetta comes from *abbrustolire,* "to brown or toast" slices of bread on a hot grill. Outside Tuscany, any toasted bread with topping, most commonly tomatoes, is called bruschetta. **PER 4 PERSONE**

4 large slices Tuscan-style or dense country-style bread
2 cloves garlic, halved, for rubbing
1 cup (250 mL) best-quality extra-virgin olive oil
Salt, QB

Grill your bread and, while it's still hot, rub fresh garlic on it. The heat actually melts the garlic right onto the bread. Then drizzle with the best olive oil you have. Remember, Tuscan bread is unsalted, so if you're using that kind of bread, do what the Tuscans do and finish with a healthy pinch of salt.

Un' altra idea: And, of course, if you want tomato on it, cut some cherry tomatoes in half and squeeze them on top, then finish with a drizzle of olive oil.

CARCIOFI Artichokes

I remember the first time I saw how artichokes grow. I was driving along the coast in Sicily. On one side of me was the beautiful blue sea, and on the other was a field of artichokes. Seeing a field of these thistles is an incredible and surreal sight. The artichoke is an otherworldly but beautiful plant. With a heavy head growing on a thin stem as high as four or five feet, it seems to defy the laws of gravity. That's how I think of the artichoke—unusual, kind of misunderstood, but very sensual.

It always surprises people when I tell them that I consider the artichoke sensual, because its outward appearance makes it look inedible. But steaming the leaves with a little garlic, olive oil and mint, then delicately pulling each one off the choke and sliding it through your teeth to get the little bit of silky meat is a sensual experience.

How to Prepare Artichokes

The artichoke may look odd and intimidating, but it's easy to prepare. And this is definitely a case when practice makes perfect. The more you do it, the more you'll learn the difference between the hard inedible petals that have to be discarded and the ones that are edible.

The first thing you should do is fill a big bowl with water. Cut two lemons in half and squeeze the juice into the bowl.

Give your artichokes a rinse under running water. Pull off the exterior hard leaves until you get to the petals that are a pale yellow-green color. With a paring knife, cut off the bottom half of the stalk, then with a knife or vegetable peeler, take off the first layer of skin to get to the pale yellow flesh. Do the same for the base of the choke. Then cut about 1/2 inch (1 cm) off the top to remove the rough, sharp tips. That's it.

Now you can either throw the artichoke right into the lemon water or do what I do: once the artichoke is cleaned, I rub it inside the lemon half, covering it with juice. The acidity from the juice prevents it from turning brown. Let each artichoke sit in the water while you clean the rest.

At this point, the artichokes can be used in a salad, on crostini or as part of a pasta sauce. You can boil, steam or grill them, or slice them into thin pieces to create one of my favorite dishes, carciofi fritti.

CARCIOFI FRITTI
Fried Tender Artichokes

There are a few different ways to fry artichokes. Some recipes call for them to be fried whole. But others, like this one, are more *sfizioso*, because they're cut into small pieces, battered and fried. They can be served hot or cold. Either way, they're to die for. **PER 6 PERSONE**

8 artichokes, cleaned and peeled (see page 68)
Extra-virgin olive oil, for frying
2 eggs, beaten
Salt, QB
All-purpose flour, for dredging

If your artichokes have been sitting in lemon water, remove them. With a paper towel or dishtowel, pat dry. You want them to be very dry. Cut them in half lengthwise and then in half again. Make sure each slice has some of the stem attached, which will prevent the artichoke slice from falling apart.

In a frying pan, heat some extra-virgin olive oil until very hot.

In one bowl, beat together the eggs and some salt. Place the flour in a second bowl. Dip each artichoke slice into the beaten egg, letting some of the excess drip off, then dredge it in the flour, coating well.

When the oil is hot, gently add the artichoke slices and fry them on both sides for a few minutes or until golden. Transfer them to a paper towel–lined plate to drain. Salt them while they're still hot.

You can eat these hot or cold. They travel well, so they're great for picnics.

ARANCINI A TRE MODI
Rice Balls Three Ways

The Sicilians get the credit for creating arancini. The name means "little oranges," because when cooked, these stuffed rice balls take on a slightly orange color. This is Italian street food, or fast food that is portable and usually eaten as a snack, which is why this recipe is in the Sfizi section. But, of course, you can have them as a meal. Arancini are easy to make. Some recipes call for making a risotto first, but here's a quick and easy version.

My three favorite fillings are mozzarella, meat and peas, and eggplant with cherry tomatoes. In all three versions you can keep the rice balls al bianco, with just the filling in the middle, or you can use tomato sauce to color and flavor the rice. I like to make my arancini con mozzarella with Salsa di Cinque Minuti di Mia Mamma, but I leave it out for the others. Either way is fine; you can't go wrong. Except for this one difference, the method for stuffing and cooking is the same for all of them. The most basic version is the mozzarella, as follows.

PER 6 PERSONE

2 cups (500 mL) Arborio rice
2 cups (500 mL) Salsa di Cinque Minuti di Mia Mamma (optional) (see page 171)
1 cup (250 mL) finely grated Parmigiano-Reggiano cheese
3 oz (90 g) mozzarella cheese, cubed
1 egg, beaten
1 cup (250 mL) dry bread crumbs
2 cups (500 mL) extra-virgin olive oil

In a pot of boiling salted water, cook the Arborio as you would any rice. Some recipes call for a two-to-one ratio of water to rice. I prefer to put the rice in the pot and pour in enough water to cover it by a couple of inches. When the rice is ready, I drain off the excess water. For my arancini con mozzarella, I mix the rice with tomato sauce. So, if you want to do this too, get out another pot while the rice is cooking and make Salsa di Cinque Minuti di Mia Mamma. When the rice is done, drain the excess water and add the rice to the pot with the tomato sauce and give it all a good stir.

Whether you choose to keep the rice al bianco or to mix it with tomato sauce, you'll want to add a good handful of Parmigiano. At this point, if you're feeling hungry, you can actually pull out a bowl and have some rice for lunch! It's to die for—and anyway, you need something to do while the rest of the rice cools down.

When the rice is cool enough to handle, scoop out a handful and roll it into a ball. You can make arancini as large or as small as you want. The small ones are a great cocktail-party finger food. The large ones allow you to put in more stuffing.

Now for the stuffing: Press a hole in the middle of the rice ball with your thumb and place a few cubes of mozzarella inside. (If you're using using one of the other fillings, use a spoon to help you stuff the centers.) Reshape the rice ball until the cheese (or your chosen filling) is fully enclosed.

One of my favorite things about arancini is that they have two different textures: the crunchy outside and the moist inside. That contrast is achieved by giving them a crust using bread crumbs. So dip each rice ball into the beaten egg, then roll it in the bread crumbs to coat it evenly. If you want to freeze some balls for later, now is the time to do it.

Pan-fry the arancini in about a 1/2 inch (1 cm) of hot olive oil until golden brown on all sides. If you have a deep-fryer, you can just plop them in and remove them when they're done. Remember, the rice is already cooked, so you're only frying them to achieve a golden color and crispness. Remove and drain on paper towels. Serve hot or at room temperature.

For my other favorite versions, substitute one of the following cooked fillings for the mozzarella and continue as above.

Meat and Pea Filling

2 tbsp (30 mL) extra-virgin olive oil
1/2 pound (250 g) lean ground beef
1/2 cup (125 mL) peas, cooked
1 cup (250 mL) Salsa di Cinque Minuti di Mia Mamma (page 171)
salt, QB

Heat up the olive oil and sauté the beef. When it's cooked, add the peas and the Salsa di Cinque Minuti di Mia Mamma and let it all cook for a few more minutes together. Add a little salt. Remove from the heat and let cool.

Eggplant and Cherry Tomato Filling

1 cup (250 mL) extra-virgin olive oil, divided
1 medium-sized eggplant, cubed
10 cherry tomatoes, quartered
salt, QB

Reserve 3 to 4 tablespoons (45 to 60 mL) of the olive oil. Heat the rest up in a high-sided frying pan. When the pan is hot, fry the eggplant until golden and crispy. Drain on paper towels. In a separate frying pan, heat up reserved olive oil, and sauté the cherry tomatoes until they soften and start to lose their shape. Add in the eggplant, a pinch of salt and cook for a minute or two. Remove from heat and let cool.

Un' altra idea: You can use any type of leftover risotto for arancini. Some risottos, like mushroom, have enough going on already, so you'd be fine not stuffing them and just going to the egg and bread crumb stage. I encourage you to be imaginative because, truthfully, I've loved every version of arancini I've ever had. I can't imagine anyone making a bad rice ball.

PER 6 PERSONE

FIORI DI ZUCCHINE
Stuffed Zucchini Flowers

When I was growing up in Toronto, not many people knew that you could actually eat the flower that comes from the zucchini plant. I would go with my mom to get our produce from a local farmer who couldn't believe that we ate the bright yellow flowers, so he'd give them to us for free. Boy, was I embarrassed! I felt that he looked at us as poor immigrants, and imagined he was thinking, "Those Italians are really strange." But eventually, he caught on to how good fiori di zucchine were, and our days of getting them for free were over. **PER 4 PERSONE**

12 zucchini flowers
1/2 cup (125 mL) all-purpose flour
1/2 cup (125 mL) white wine
1 egg, beaten
1 large ball fresh mozzarella, cut into thin strips
12 anchovies
Extra-virgin olive oil, for frying
Salt, QB

The flowers are easy to clean, but remember they are very, very delicate, so do *not* rinse them under water. Use a clean dry dish cloth to wipe off any dirt, and take a look inside to make sure they're clean.

To make the batter: Pour the flour into a bowl and add the wine. You don't want the batter to be too runny or too thick. Mix well with a fork, pressing down to get rid of any lumps. Then whisk in the egg.

At this point, you could just batter and fry the fiori di zucchine; they taste great on their own. But why stop there? In Rome, zucchini flowers are always stuffed with mozzarella and anchovies, and that's how I like them. Avoid the temptation of overstuffing them, though. Fill them gently. Don't worry if the cheese sticks out a bit; the batter will cover everything and act as a seal.

In a frying pan, heat about 1 inch (2.5 cm) of extra-virgin olive oil over high heat. It's very important that the oil be really hot, so the flowers get crisp and don't absorb the oil.

Dip the stuffed flowers in the batter, making sure they're fully coated, and shake off any excess. Once the oil is hot, very gently lower the flowers into the pan and fry them on all sides until they're nice and golden. Take them out and place them on paper towels to absorb the excess oil, then sprinkle with salt.

FRICO
Parmigiano Chips

This is a sophisticated little chip that seems to work perfectly with prosecco or champagne. The first time I had them was in Friuli. They were served just before dinner with a chilled glass of prosecco. It beautifully set the tone for the whole night. The good news is that they're very simple to make. You literally need one ingredient: Parmigiano-Reggiano cheese. **PER 4 PERSONE**

3 cups (750 mL) Parmigiano-Reggiano cheese, some finely grated and some coarsely grated, combined

Begin by heating a frying pan on medium-high heat. Don't put any oil in the pan as there's enough in the cheese. Sprinkle the Parmigiano in the pan in a thin, even layer so that the cheese covers the surface. Just make sure you don't put too much in. You want the frico to be thin and crispy.

As it cooks, you'll see it start to bubble, and the cheese will break down into a semi-liquid state. Keep an eye on it: if the pan begins to smoke, turn down the heat to medium. Once the cheese has melted together, just slide it out of the frying pan onto a plate. Help it along with your spatula if you need to, making sure it stays flat and doesn't fold over onto itself.

Allow it to cool down and completely solidify, which only takes about a minute. Break it up with your hands into little chips. Now you have a perfect finger food, beautifully crunchy and salty, like a chip.

Un' altra idea: Try this recipe as a substitute for croutons in a salad or use it to form cheese baskets for serving your mixed greens. To create baskets, instead of transferring the cheese to a plate, simply slide the melted Parmigiano down over an inverted coffee cup and let it set. In a few minutes, you'll be able to remove it, and you'll have a Parmigiano cheese basket to serve with a green salad inside.

SALVIA FRITTA CON ACCIUGHE
Fried Sage Leaves with Anchovies

This is one of my favorite cocktail snacks. The anchovies are sandwiched between two sage leaves and then fried. The resulting little bite is surprisingly meaty and satisfying. You can also eliminate the anchovies and just fry the sage leaves. If you've never had fried sage leaves, you must try them—they're a real treat. Both versions go especially well with a chilled glass of white wine or prosecco.

These should be enjoyed hot and crispy. They're great to serve at a house party, with your guests hanging out in the kitchen while you make them. Most people don't think you can fry sage, so when they taste this, I guarantee they're going to be blown away. For this recipe, it's really important that you use big sage leaves.   **PER 4 PERSONE**

Extra-virgin olive oil, for frying
12 anchovies
24 large fresh sage leaves
1 egg, beaten
All-purpose flour, for dredging
Salt, QB

Pour olive oil into a frying pan to a depth of about 1 inch (2.5 cm). Heat on medium-high heat. To test if it's hot enough, drop in a bit of the egg; if it sizzles, the oil is ready. Be careful—olive oil can smoke if it gets too hot.

Place an anchovy fillet between 2 large sage leaves. It's really important that you use large leaves because you want to enclose the anchovy to resemble a little panino. Dip the little panino into the beaten egg. Be sure to let the excess drip off before you dredge it in the flour. Shake off the excess flour to ensure you get a light batter. This isn't a fish stick! Repeat with remaining sage leaves and anchovies.

Put as many sage panini into the hot oil as will fit without overcrowding. After a few minutes, flip them over. When they become golden brown and crisp, transfer them to a paper towel–lined plate to drain. Sprinkle with salt. I salt my fried foods right out of the fryer, nice and hot. That way, the salt sticks. Serve immediately.

PIZZA FRITTA
Fried Dough

Let me be perfectly honest with you: *pizza fritta* is "fried dough." Unfortunately, in translation it loses its romance and doesn't sound healthy, but trust me, it's a snack to die for.

At your next informal party, bring your guests into the kitchen, crack open a bottle of wine, and get them involved. To me, it's sensual because you get to play with the dough and make your own pizzas. And any recipe that gets people cooking together, with results that taste this good, will make your gathering special.

This is also a great way to get the children in your life into the kitchen. I remember coming home from school, and my *nonna* would have already prepared pizza dough. That was one of the ways I was introduced to cooking, because what kid doesn't love playing with dough? And when the final product tastes this good, your kid is going to feel empowered, just like I was. Of course, you may not have an Italian grandmother preparing your dough, so it's okay to buy it ready-made from the bakery or the supermarket.

Here are two versions: one is savory, with a simple tomato sauce, and the second is sweet and complex, with a combination of honey and pecorino cheese. Both are simple and quick to whip up.   **PER 4 PERSONE**

For the dough:
1 lb (500 g) pizza dough
Extra-virgin olive oil, for frying

To make the sweet version:
2 tbsp (30 mL) liquid honey
Freshly grated pecorino cheese, QB (optional)

For the tomato sauce:
1 can (14 oz/398 mL) crushed tomatoes
Salt, QB
2 cloves garlic, cut into large chunks
1/4 cup (50 mL) extra-virgin olive oil
Fresh basil leaves, QB
Freshly grated pecorino cheese, QB

For the tomato sauce: This is almost like making a tomato sauce backwards! It will give you a fresh, almost raw tomato taste that works perfectly on the fried dough and with the pecorino. To start, pour the crushed tomatoes into a pan and then add some salt. Now throw in the garlic. Leave the garlic in big chunks because you're going to remove them before you put the sauce on the pizza. Add the olive oil and bring the sauce to a light bubble. It only needs to cook for a few minutes. You can tear up some raw basil and throw it in at this point, or save the whole leaves to arrange on each pizza along with the grated pecorino.

Cut up the dough into little strips and start working it with your hands, stretching and shaping it outward so that you end up with little discs about the size of your hand, give or take.

Now pour a generous amount of olive oil into a frying pan, to a depth of 1 to 2 inches (2.5 to 5 cm), depending on the number of pizzas you're making. It's important that your oil be really hot so that the dough gets crispy and doesn't absorb too much grease.

Gently lay your dough discs in the oil. If cooking more than one at a time, make sure they're spaced out in the pan; don't overcrowd them. Fry until the discs become fluffy and airy, puffing up before your eyes. The crust will look crispy and golden brown. Remove them carefully and place on a paper towel to absorb the oil.

To make your pizzas, spoon some of the fresh tomato sauce on each, making sure you don't include any of the garlic pieces. Add the basil (if not already added to the sauce) and pecorino. You can also use Parmigiano-Reggiano, but the pecorino has a sharp bite that contrasts nicely with the sweet tomato sauce.

For a sweet version: Drizzle honey on the fried dough. You can eat it as is or, as I like to, with a sprinkle of pecorino cheese.

CROCCHETTE DI PATATE
Potato Croquettes

I love potatoes in any size, shape or form. Give me a potato recipe, and I'm a happy boy! I think of these croquettes as portable mashed potatoes—crispy on the outside, luxuriously creamy on the inside. When you bite into them, *o Dio*! It's an explosion of textures and flavors: the crisp outside, the creamy Parmigiano mashed potato and then, *finalmente,* the taleggio oozing with cheesy goodness. I've never met a potato croquette I didn't like! If you fall in love with this dish and want to make extra, freeze them before you fry them. They'll hold well in the freezer for that rainy day when you need some potato love.   **PER 4 PERSONE**

1 1/4 lb (625 g) potatoes
7 oz (200 g) taleggio or fresh mozzarella cheese
1/2 cup (125 mL) freshly grated
   Parmigiano-Reggiano cheese
1/2 cup (125 mL) finely chopped fresh flat-leaf parsley

2 eggs, beaten separately
Salt and freshly ground pepper, QB
Dry bread crumbs, QB
Sesame seeds, QB
Extra-virgin olive oil, for frying

Peel the potatoes and cook them in a large pot of boiling salted water until fork-tender. Drain and set aside to cool a bit. While the potatoes relax, cut the taleggio into thin strips; set aside. When the potatoes are cool enough to handle, mash them. I like to use a potato press or potato ricer, because I think it gives the croquettes a better texture, but you can also use a large fork.

For the next step, it's important to make sure your potatoes are really cool. Otherwise, when you add your egg and cheese, the heat of the potatoes will cook everything and you'll end up with a bad potato frittata. So, into a mixing bowl go the mashed potatoes, Parmigiano, parsley, one of the eggs, and salt and pepper. Now is the time to add more salt, pepper or Parmigiano, if needed.

Next comes the fun part. Get your hands in there and mix everything up. When it's well combined, scoop out a handful, lay a strip of taleggio in the middle of the mixture and roll up to form a potato log with cheese in the middle. My mouth is watering already. Keep going until all the potato mixture and cheese strips are used up. For the croquette coating, dip the logs into the remaining beaten egg, shaking off the excess, and roll in the bread crumbs, then the sesame seeds.

Pour 1 to 2 inches (2.5 to 5 cm) of extra-virgin olive oil into a pan and heat it up. It's important the oil be really hot, so the croquettes don't absorb it but become nice and crisp on the outside and deliciously creamy on the inside. Fry the croquettes until golden brown on all sides. Since the potatoes are already cooked, it takes only a few minutes. Drain on paper towels.

Un' altra idea: These can be shaped into little balls, like arancini. They also make a great cocktail snack.

MOZZARELLA IN CARROZZA
Mozzarella in a Carriage

This classic Neapolitan snack is Italy's version of the grilled cheese sandwich. It's really a cross between grilled cheese and French toast. But, I promise you, it's better than both. The star ingredient is fresh mozzarella. You want the freshest and creamiest mozzarella you can get your hands on. You'll find it in the deli section of the supermarket in a tray of water, or packaged in a container with water.

Now the bread. While it may seem a bit contradictory, considering that Italian bread is usually so rustic and full of flavor, you want to go for white bread in this recipe. I recommend removing the crust because it makes the whole sandwich softer and more delicate.   **PER 4 PERSONE**

1 cup (250 mL) milk
2 eggs
1 large ball fresh mozzarella, sliced
4 anchovies
8 slices white bread, crusts removed
2 tbsp (30 mL) extra-virgin olive oil
Salt, QB

Whisk together the milk and eggs.

Sandwich a slice of mozzarella and an anchovy fillet between 2 slices of bread to create the "carriage." Anchovies are optional, but I like the slightly salty shock against the delicate, neutral flavor of the cheese. Repeat this to make a total of 4 sandwiches. Then put your frying pan on the burner over medium-high heat and add the olive oil.

Here comes the French toast part of the recipe: Dip the sandwiches into the egg mixture so both sides are fully coated. In batches, place them in the heated frying pan and cook, turning once, until both sides are golden brown. Add a light sprinkle of salt (not too much because the anchovies are a little salty) and serve immediately.

Leftovers

Why leftovers? I'm passionate about leftovers!

In fact, I don't understand why people throw food out. I'll sometimes deliberately make extra of certain dishes because (a) some taste even better the next day, or (b) I need the leftovers to form the basis of a completely new dish. It's also very *dolce vita* because even in the midst of abundance, it reflects a consciousness, a respect for the food.

That said, leftovers are about comfort, too. When I was a kid, I remember wanting to come home for lunch, especially when my mom had made a great meal the night before and I knew there were leftovers.

Here are some of my favorites. I encourage you to try them, and then create your own. A little *fantasia* goes a long way in the kitchen. It's about reinvention, transformation, artistry and a little *dolce vita*.

PASTA FRITTA
Best Damn Leftover Pasta Dish Ever a.k.a. Fried Pasta

When I was in grade school, I was king of my lunchroom because this is what my mom would pack for me. Of course, I knew she was just using up leftovers from last night's dinner, but I didn't care. It looked and tasted better than the bologna sandwiches my mates had. Now it's a habit for me to always make extra spaghetti so I can make this recipe the next day.

If you're a first-time cook, this recipe is a great place to start. In fact, I have a few friends who decided to learn how to cook after watching me make this and tasting it. They couldn't believe how simple it was and how amazing it tasted.

Leftover spaghetti, eggs, salt, freshly grated Parmigiano-Reggiano cheese and extra-virgin olive oil

You can use any leftover pasta you like, but I strongly recommend spaghetti because the individual strands seem to crisp up better. I like my pasta fritta thin and flattened out like a pizza. My mom makes a thicker version, so it's really up to you. And by the way, the answer is yes—your leftover pastas should already have been mixed with your tomato sauce.

In a large mixing bowl, beat an egg or two. Add a little bit of salt, but just a bit because your pasta is already flavored. This is totally optional, but if you want to add a handful of freshly grated Parmigiano, go ahead, then give it a good stir. Next, add your leftover spaghetti and mix well so that the pasta is fully coated in the egg mixture. That's what's going to keep your pasta fritta intact.

Now pour a good amount of olive oil into a hot frying pan. I recommend using a nonstick pan for this. Once your oil is hot, pour in the egg and spaghetti mixture, spreading it so that it's nice and flat in your pan. Cook it for about 5 minutes or until the bottom gets crisp. To flip it over, cover it with a plate larger than the pan and carefully flip them together to invert the fried spaghetti onto the plate. Then slide it back into the pan and cook until crisp and golden brown.

FRITTATA DI VERDURA
Clean-out-the-Fridge Frittata

I put this in my leftover section, not so much because it's a leftover meal, but because this is a great way to use vegetables that have seen better days. You know what I mean: vegetables that are shrivelled up or wilting.

The same is true of ingredients like cheese or prosciutto. I can't tell you how many times I haven't wrapped them properly and they've become hard and dried out. That's when they're perfect for this kind of recipe.

A good frittata should have a sautéed white onion as its base. From there, you can really use any other vegetable, so grab what you have on hand and go to town. A frittata is also great in the dead of winter when there isn't much fresh produce. But with a bag of frozen peas, an onion, some prosciutto and eggs, you have a frittata con piselli.

The irony is that this dish itself makes a good leftover. The next day you can turn your frittata into a sandwich or serve it as part of an antipasto. Of course, you don't have to make this dish with leftovers or with vegetables that are going bad, but it's a clever way to use ingredients that are past their prime. It's alchemy.

In a bowl, whisk 6 to 8 eggs. If you have any dried-out cheese you want to use, cut it into cubes and add it to the eggs. Put the sautéed vegetables and/or prosciutto into the bowl with the egg mixture and immediately pour them back into the frying pan. You might have to add a little olive oil to the pan so the eggs don't stick, especially if you're not using a nonstick pan. I'll leave that up to your judgment. Let it cook on medium heat for a few minutes while the eggs set. Then set a lid or oversized plate over the whole pan and let the dish finish cooking.

Some of my favorite combinations are potatoes and onions; onions and peppers; zucchini and onions.

PER 4–6 PERSONE

SPINACI SALTATE
Sautéed Spinach

This contorno is so basic that I'm not even going to give you measurements. It's a staple in most Italian restaurants, and you can ask for it even if it's not on the menu—no one will bat an eyelash. Some nights this, with a piece of rustic fresh bread, Parmigiano and a glass of wine, is all I want.

Wash a bunch of spinach. You don't have time to wash spinach, or it's the dead of winter? Fine, use frozen. Now, heat up a good amount of extra-virgin olive oil in a frying pan. Brown some sliced or minced garlic—it's up to you. Add some chili flakes and then throw in your fresh or defrosted spinach. Sauté everything and add some salt. Within minutes you'll be wondering why spinach doesn't have a better reputation.

ZUCCHINE ALLA SCAPECE
Zucchini Finished in Vinegar

Alla scapece is another cooking method that shows off the Italians' inventiveness and their love of food. It's a throwback to the days before refrigeration, when people used to preserve their foods in a vinegar-based dressing.

The method can be used to preserve many types of vegetables and fish, especially cod. Sometimes you'll need to cook the ingredients first, but other times the acidity of the vinegar itself is enough to "cook" the food.

In the late summer or early fall, when you have lots of great vegetables, you can use the scapece method to make your own preserves. Simply cut cauliflower, zucchini, eggplant, broccoli or carrots into small pieces and boil them until they're fork-tender. After you've drained them, add garlic, olive oil and vinegar, and seal them in sterilized, airtight jars. You can enjoy them months later. In this recipe I deep-fry the zucchini first, for a little crunch. **PER 4 PERSONE**

5 small zucchini, thinly sliced
Splash water
1 cup (250 mL) all-purpose flour
Extra-virgin olive oil, for frying
Salt, QB
Splash white wine vinegar

The secret here is to moisten the zucchini slices slightly, so that the flour sticks to them. Put them in a bowl and, using your fingers, sprinkle on some water. Then get your hands in there and toss the slices until all of them are moistened.

Put the flour in a separate bowl and roll the zucchini slices in it, using a light touch. You don't want a heavy batter, so shake off any excess flour. Heat the olive oil, and fry the zucchini until golden.

Drain the slices on a plate lined with paper towels, salt them while they're still hot, and finish with a splash of white wine vinegar. Serve hot.

LENTICCHIE CON PANCETTA
Sautéed Lentils with Pancetta

This is one of those last-minute quick-and-easy dishes you can make with pantry staples. It definitely beats grabbing a pizza or a burger on your way home from work. It's simple, and you'll feel so much better. It's also a very comforting dish. You can have it as a side, or you can turn it into a soup just by adding water or stock.

I always have a couple of cans of lentils in my cupboard for what I call "emergency meals." But you can substitute beans or chickpeas, if you like. If you have time, you can also use dried legumes, but the reality is that we don't always have time for that. And this dish is so good that sometimes I just want it when I want it!

Instead of pancetta, you can use gambuccio, which is the end of the prosciutto leg. It's much less expensive than pancetta slices and tastes the same. It gives loads of flavor, but just isn't as pretty. Alternatively, if you have any dried-out prosciutto or salami slices that have been in your fridge for a few days and you're thinking about throwing them out, don't! They're great natural flavor enhancers. Just cube them and fry them up as a base for your dish.   **PER 4 PERSONE**

9 oz (275 g) pancetta
1 white cooking onion
1 clove garlic
1/2 cup (125 mL) extra-virgin olive oil
1 sprig fresh rosemary
Chili pepper flakes, QB
2 cans (each 19 oz/540 mL) brown lentils
Salt, QB

Start by dicing up your pancetta, onion and garlic. Heat up a pan and add the olive oil. Cook the garlic, onions, pancetta, rosemary, and chili flakes until everything begins to turn golden. I like to cook everything together so that I'll even have crisp bits of rosemary. If you're using canned lentils, drain them, rinse under cold water and throw them into the pan. Cook for a few minutes to flavor the lentils. Taste, salt, and—*basta*—you're done!

RADICCHIO ALLA GRIGLIA
Grilled Radicchio

Radicchio is one of my favorite greens—even though it's not actually green. It's a gorgeous marbled ruby-colored lettuce with a slightly bitter taste. It's also a tougher leaf than most of its green counterparts, which means it stands up to a lot of treatments. You can throw it raw into a salad to add color and bite. You can season it in advance, and it won't wilt like other greens. And it works well on the grill and in the oven. It stands up to the cooking and takes on a wonderful, almost smoky flavor. One note: Make sure your barbecue or grill is not too hot. You want a medium heat, so the radicchio doesn't burn.

Radicchio shrinks when it's cooked, so make a bit more than you think you need. The bonus is that if there's any left over, it tastes great served cold from the fridge or at room temperature.

There are different types of radicchio: one is small, round and about the size of a bocce ball, and the other is long, leafy and slightly more bitter in taste. Radicchio is a hardy vegetable and grows well in colder climates. My mom used to grow it in her garden in Toronto and would harvest it well into October and sometimes even November.

PER 4 PERSONE

2 heads radicchio
Salt and freshly ground pepper, QB
1/4 cup (50 mL) extra-virgin olive oil
1/4 cup (50 mL) balsamic vinegar

Cut your radicchio in half, then in quarters. There's always the temptation to cut off the end; I recommend you don't, because that little piece will actually hold the radicchio wedge in place. Before you put it on the grill, season it with a little salt and pepper, and a good splash each of extra-virgin olive oil and balsamic vinegar. At this point, you can let it sit if you want the seasoning to get a little deeper into the radicchio, but it's not necessary. Place it on a medium-hot grill and cook for a few minutes on each side or until it gets charred and soft. Keep an eye on things; radicchio burns very quickly.

If you don't have a barbecue, you can slow-roast the radicchio. Arrange the wedges on a baking sheet, season and roast in a 400°F (200°C) oven for about 15 minutes.

FINOCCHIO AL FORNO
Caramelized Fennel

Fennel is one of those unusual-looking vegetables that seem to stump a lot of people, and so they pass it by at the supermarket. There's nothing to be scared of. It's incredibly easy to prepare and has a wonderful, unusual, slightly licorice flavor. It's also really good for digestion. My mother used to serve it raw after a big meal because, as she would say, *"Ti aiuta a digerire dopo il pranzo"*—it helps digestion after a meal. Whether you serve it raw in a salad, or slow-roasted in an oven, where it becomes soft and caramelized, fennel is a versatile vegetable. **PER 4 PERSONE**

2 large fennel bulbs
6 tbsp (90 mL) extra-virgin olive oil
1/2 cup (125 mL) freshly grated Parmigiano-Reggiano cheese
Salt and freshly ground pepper, QB
1/2 cup (125 mL) dry bread crumbs

To clean the fennel, rinse it, then cut off and discard the long stalks. You now have a heart-shaped bulb. I like to cut that into eighths—the smaller the pieces, the shorter the cooking time.

Drop the cleaned fennel into a pot of boiling salted water and cook for about 5 minutes or until just fork-tender. Don't go too crazy at this point. You're just giving it a head start so that it cuts the cooking time in the oven. When you take the fennel out of the pot, it's really important that you remove as much water as possible. You might even want to pat it dry with paper towels. That way, it will roast more quickly.

Spread your dried fennel in the roasting pan and add lots of love in the form of olive oil, some freshly grated Parmigiano, salt and pepper. Sprinkle with bread crumbs and cook in a 450°F (230°C) oven for about 30 minutes or until caramelized and a nice golden color. This recipe is very forgiving—the longer you cook it, the more caramelized, sweet and tasty it gets.

PATATE AL FORNO
Roasted Potatoes

I don't know many people who don't like roasted potatoes. This is one of those universal dishes, and it's so simple to make. In fact, if your kids are old enough to handle some chopping duties, this is a great thing for them to do while you prepare something else. Once the potatoes are cut up, you're done—the oven will take care of the rest. This dish is also a great way to use up odds and ends. For example, if you have a tomato that needs to be used, just chop it up and throw it in. Or if you have dried-out Parmigiano cheese or the rinds, dice them up and throw them in as well. The results are addictive.

Fresh herbs are an important part of this recipe. In Italy, most people have a small herb garden or a couple of herb plants in a window box next to the kitchen so that, as they cook, they can snip off what they need. If you have a sunny windowsill in your kitchen, I recommend doing the same. Otherwise, your local supermarket or greengrocer likely has a good selection of fresh herbs year-round. For this recipe, I like to use fresh thyme, rosemary and sage. If you're making a last-minute dish to use up potatoes and you don't have all of these herbs, don't be too worried. Rosemary is the only one that I think is a must.

PER 4 PERSONE

1 1/2 lb (750 g) Yukon gold potatoes
Fresh thyme, sage and rosemary, QB
2 cloves garlic, chopped
1/2 cup (125 mL) extra-virgin olive oil
Salt, QB

Peel the potatoes and cut them into wedges. Give the herbs a rough chop. I sometimes leave the sprig of rosemary whole and just put it on top. Arrange the potatoes in a roasting pan and sprinkle with the herbs. Throw in the garlic, then add quite a bit of extra-virgin olive oil and salt. This is a case when I recommend being liberal with salt. Potatoes absorb it well, and the dish won't become too salty, just very tasty. Toss well to season all the potatoes. Roast in a 400°F (200°C) oven for about 40 minutes or until golden.

The Coffee Bar

The coffee bar is the social hub of every Italian neighborhood. After leaving the house, most Italians stop at their local bar for their first cappuccino or coffee of the day. It's not because they can't make it at home—it's a social ritual.

No one sits down. You order at the bar and stand there bantering with the *barista* and the other regulars. And anyone and everyone throws in comments about last night's game, the latest political news or a celebrity's latest gaffe. After a while, you become one of the locals, a fixture. And don't be surprised if someone else buys your espresso—it's the Italian way. Treating someone, even a stranger, is considered a pleasure. And as with all true acts of generosity, no one keeps score. There's no obligation. It's done with an open heart.

You'll rarely see anyone carrying out a Styrofoam or paper cup. Most Italians drink their coffee at the bar. If you decide you want to take a coffee to a friend, you'll find it given to you in an empty juice bottle that's been washed out and kept for that exact purpose. Glass doesn't rob the coffee of its flavor. Or, if you're a regular, the *barista* will offer you a tray with two proper coffee cups. To a serious coffee drinker, drinking from Styrofoam or a waxed cardboard cup is blasphemy!

It's an ordinary activity, but one of the great pleasures of Italian life. Truly *dolce vita*.

Insalate

Italian salads are not always leafy salads. Sometimes they're a simple combination of a few ingredients chosen for their contrasting colors or textures and brought together with a fantastic extra-virgin olive oil. This is the time when you break out the best bottle in the kitchen. A little goes a long way. And I never sit down to eat a salad without a great piece of bread.

SOME ASSEMBLY REQUIRED

Part of me is almost a little embarrassed about including the next few recipes in the book. There's not much to them, and, in fact, it borders on the ridiculous to call some of them recipes. You cut up some tomatoes, slice up some mozzarella, tear up a little basil, add salt and drizzle on the best extra-virgin olive oil in your kitchen. Or slice up some oranges and balance the sweetness and color with contrasting tastes and textures, like sharp red onions, salty olives and anchovies. These are recipes? Well, when you taste them, you'll know why I've included them here.

The Tuscan salad pinzimonio is really an assortment of raw vegetables that you just dip into a bowl of the finest extra-virgin olive oil, fresh from the olive harvest. Could it be simpler? You wash the vegetables, cut them up, then dip them into the oil. Enjoy pinzimonio with a bunch of people, and see if you don't end up having a perfect *dolce vita* moment. It's the alchemy, the magic, that happens with great ingredients. This chapter, more than any other in the book, is an example of what I've been saying—that you can create magical meals with just a few simple ingredients in a short time. Please use the best extra-virgin olive oil you can get your hands on. There's a reason why it's considered the oil of the gods. It's liquid gold. You can actually create masterpieces with great olive oil.

COLAZIONE DEL CONTADINO
Farmer's Breakfast

This rustic dish is another example of *cucina povera.* It originated in Sicily, where the farmers would get up before the sun, work until mid-morning, then take a break to have their breakfast, usually using what they grew themselves. This dish is surprisingly hearty, and if you make it when tomatoes are at their peak and use terrific olive oil, you might, like me, end up having it for breakfast, lunch and dinner.

PER 4 PERSONE

8 ripe tomatoes, quartered
1 clove garlic
1/2 red onion, chopped
Freshly squeezed lemon juice, salt and extra-virgin olive oil, QB
Splash water

Using a pestle, bash up the quartered tomatoes and garlic in a large bowl. When the mixture looks like it's been run over by a Vespa, add the chopped red onion, a good squeeze of lemon juice, some salt, a generous amount of olive oil and a splash of water. Let this stand for about 10 minutes and then remove the garlic. There will be a lot of liquid at the bottom, which is a good thing.

Years ago, farmers would place stale bread on a plate and dump all the ingredients over the bread to make their own version of a morning crostini. My point is that this dish is so good you could either have it with stale bread or eat it as a main-course salad with some fresh country-style bread *per fare la scarpetta*—to mop up all that flavorful liquid. It will taste incredible either way.

INSALATA DEL CONTADINO
Sicilian Farmer's Salad

I came across this salad in Sicily, where the fruits and olive oils are rich with intense flavor thanks to the beautiful Mediterranean climate. Who would have thought that fruit and olive oil would work so well together? This recipe calls for a lemon. Sicilian lemons are less tart and even slightly sweet. If you can't find Sicilian lemons, you may want to reduce the quantity, or not use lemons at all. You'll be surprised at the way all the contrasting flavors come together in this salad. **PER 4 PERSONE**

1 orange
1 lemon
2 small cantaloupes
Salt, freshly squeezed lemon juice and extra-virgin olive oil, QB

Peel and cube your fruit, making sure you remove and discard all the rinds. Put them together in a big bowl. Add some salt and freshly squeezed lemon juice. Finish it off with your good extra-virgin olive oil. This salad works well on its own with some bread, but it also makes a great accompaniment to freshly grilled meat or fish.

INSALATA CAPRESE

Probably the most famous salad in Italy, the caprese is named after the Island of Capri, where it was created. This is a perfect example of a dish that lets the ingredients do all the talking.

This recipe calls for mozzarella, but we're not talking about the stuff you shred and sprinkle on your pizza. Look for mozzarella di bufala, which is made from buffalo milk and has a particularly creamy texture. Or use fior di latte, which literally means "flower of milk." It's also creamy, but made from cow's milk and more readily available. **PER 4 PERSONE**

2 large balls fresh mozzarella
2 large tomatoes (or 12 cherry tomatoes)
4 fresh basil leaves
Extra-virgin olive oil, QB
Salt, QB

This is about as easy as it gets. Slice the mozzarella (I like mine fairly thick), then lay the slices on your serving platter. If using large tomatoes, cut them into pieces of equal size and layer them on the platter so that each is paired with a mozzarella slice. If using cherry tomatoes, you can keep about half whole and slice the rest, arranging all of them gently on top of the cheese in any way you like. Rip up the basil leaves and sprinkle them over top.

Now for the "dressing": a drizzle of your best extra-virgin olive oil and salt. *Basta!* When the ingredients are this luxuriously creamy and delicious, you don't want to bury them with strong vinegar. *É da Dio!*

INSALATA DI FARRO
Spelt Salad

I think of spelt as an idiot-proof grain. Even if you overcook it, it retains its shape and taste. It's one of the chameleons of the grain world. It can go into a soup or a salad. It can be the foundation of a hearty dish but still be light. It's firm but chewy. For a lot of people, it's still an undiscovered grain, but if you try it, I think it will become a regular part of your cooking repertoire. For this salad, you can really use any combination of vegetables you want or have on hand. And because you're not after looks here, you can even use vegetables that are on their way out or are from the reduced bin at the market. This salad works well warm, at room temperature or cold. And it holds in the fridge for a few days. In fact, the longer it sits, the better it tastes. **PER 4 PERSONE**

For the spelt:
3 tbsp (45 mL) extra-virgin olive oil
2 cloves garlic, finely chopped
3/4 lb (375 g) spelt
6 cups (1.5 L) vegetable stock,
 plus extra for sautéing vegetables

For the vegetables:
3 tbsp (45 mL) extra-virgin olive oil
1 red onion, roughly chopped
2 zucchini, sliced
1 sweet red pepper, chopped
1 eggplant, chopped
10 cherry tomatoes, halved
Salt, QB
1 bunch fresh flat-leaf parsley, finely chopped
1 small bunch fresh mint leaves, finely chopped
Walnuts or pine nuts, toasted, QB

For the spelt: Heat the olive oil in a pan over medium-high heat. Add the garlic and let it brown. Next, in goes your spelt. Stir it around to toast it, which enhances its nutty flavor. Add half of the vegetable stock and stir. Cook for about 10 minutes and check back. You want to cook the spelt in the stock, but you don't want it to be soupy, so although I've suggested 6 cups (1.5 L) here, you might need less. When the first half of the stock is absorbed, start adding more, a little at a time, until the spelt is moist and chewy. Don't worry if there's still a bit of stock in the pot.

For the vegetables: Heat the olive oil in a frying pan. Add the vegetables and some salt. Sauté until soft and caramelized. If the vegetables are cooking too fast, turn down the heat. Resist the temptation to add more oil to prevent the vegetables from sticking. Instead, add a bit more stock or even a bit of water to help them cook. Add the cooked vegetables to the pot of spelt and give it a really good mix. Remove it from the heat and toss in the parsley and mint. Mix it well so that the herbs are dispersed throughout the salad. Set it aside and let it cool.

When you're ready to serve, top with some toasted walnuts or pine nuts. Add a drizzle of extra-virgin olive oil, *e buon appetito.*

POMODORI RIPIENI
Day-at-the-Beach Stuffed Tomatoes

This is a fantastic and healthy portable snack that we used to have all the time as kids. In fact, in Italy during our summer vacations, the aunts would whip this up at the beach, mayonnaise and all. Don't be intimidated by the idea of doing the mayo from scratch. It's a simple version that takes minutes to make, and it's lighter, more delicate and so much better than the store-bought stuff. Whether you're in your kitchen or at the seaside, the flavor it adds is worth it.

PER 4 PERSONE

For the mayonnaise:
3 egg yolks
1 cup (250 mL) extra-virgin olive oil
Salt, QB
Juice of half a lemon

4 large firm tomatoes
2 cans (each 6 oz/170 g) tuna, packed in olive oil
1 bunch fresh flat-leaf parsley, finely chopped
3 tbsp (45 mL) capers, drained

To make the mayonnaise: In a bowl, start beating the egg yolks, then slowly drizzle in the extra-virgin olive oil in a thin, steady stream while whisking constantly. Keep going until the yolks and oil emulsify into a uniform mixture. Add salt and lemon juice and continue to whisk until well blended and creamy.

Cut off the top quarter of each tomato. Carefully scoop out and discard the insides with a spoon.

To make the filling: Drain the tuna and put it in a bowl along with the parsley. Chop 2 tbsp (30 mL) of the capers and add them to bowl along with three-quarters of the mayonnaise. Mix well. Spoon the mixture into the tomato shells. Top each with the remaining mayonnaise and capers.

INSALATA DI CARCIOFI
Raw Artichoke Salad

One day, I went to see my vegetable vendor, Maria, at the Mercato di Sant'Ambrogio in Florence, looking to buy some ingredients for a quick salad. She had a big, beautiful pile of the first baby artichokes of the season. She recommended I buy some, insisting they would make *"un' insalata incredibile."* I'd never heard of using raw artichokes before and thought she must be crazy, so, of course, I had to try it!

PER 4 PERSONE

4 artichokes
Juice of 1 lemon
5 tbsp (75 mL) extra-virgin olive oil
Salt and freshly ground pepper, QB
Shavings Parmigiano-Reggiano cheese

Remove all tough external leaves from the artichokes (see page 68). Discard the stem.

Cut the artichokes in half lengthwise. Lay them cut side down on a chopping board and slice them crosswise as thinly as possible. Place the slices in a bowl and season immediately with lemon juice, olive oil, and salt and pepper. Put them on a serving plate and finish with shavings of Parmigiano cheese.

Un' altra idea: Toast some bread to make crostini. Top with the artichoke salad and shave the Parmigiano over top.

CARPACCIO DI MANZO
Beef Carpaccio

Beef carpaccio is a dish associated with high-end eating, but it's really simple to make, and the payoff is that your guests will think you're a genius. The secret is to make sure you buy the best beef tenderloin you can find, preferably organic and from a butcher you trust, because it is, after all, eaten raw.

PER 4 PERSONE

12 oz (375 g) whole beef tenderloin
1 bunch arugula
Salt and freshly ground pepper, QB
Extra-virgin olive oil, for drizzling
Juice of 1 lemon
Shavings Parmigiano-Reggiano cheese
1 cup (250 mL) pomegranate seeds

About 20 minutes before you want to make this, get out your plastic wrap, wrap up the tenderloin, and put it in the freezer. You want it to freeze a bit, which will make slicing easier.

Unwrap the tenderloin and, with a chef's knife, cut slices about 1/8 inch (3 mm) thick. Put each slice between 2 pieces of plastic wrap and pound with a meat pounder until they're paper thin.

Now it's just about assembly. Lay the carpaccio on a serving platter. Rip up some arugula and sprinkle it over top. I like arugula in this dish because it adds a peppery taste. Season with salt, pepper, olive oil and lemon juice.

With a vegetable peeler, shave some Parmigiano over the carpaccio for a nice presentation. Sprinkle pomegranate seeds over the whole platter to give the dish a beautiful color and a nice hit of flavor.

INSALATA DI PERE E PARMIGIANO DI NONNO ANTONIO
My Grandfather Antonio's Parmigiano and Pear Salad

This salad is inspired by my *nonno* Antonio. When I was a child, after dinner he would bring pears and a big hunk of Parmigiano to the table on a large wooden cutting board. He'd cut a slice of pear and carve off a piece of Parmigiano and hand them to me, encouraging me to eat them together. The combination of the sweet, juicy pear and the granular, semi-sharp Parmigiano was a gift from the ingredient gods! Even when I was eight, I recognized this. This salad was inspired by that memory.

PER 4 PERSONE

2 firm pears, cored and cubed
1 bunch arugula
10 oz (300 g) Parmigiano-Reggiano cheese
Salt, QB
Extra-virgin olive oil, for drizzling
Balsamic vinegar, for drizzling
1/2 cup (125 mL) pine nuts, toasted

Core the pears, cut them into chunks and put them right into your serving bowl. Rip up the arugula and toss it into the bowl. Carve up some chunks of Parmigiano and add them as well.

Season with salt, olive oil and balsamic vinegar. I like to add some toasted pine nuts, which, for me, are a real treat. Toast the pine nuts in a dry frying pan (that means without using oil). It only takes a few minutes, so keep your eye on them, shaking the pan to move them around. Be careful because pine nuts burn very quickly. Sprinkle them on top of the salad and serve.

INSALATA DI FAGIOLI E TONNO
Tuna and Bean Salad

Okay, this is about as easy and as classic as it gets. Insalata di fagioli is a traditional Tuscan bean salad. I've added tuna because it works so well with beans. I can't tell you how many times Nina and I have come home at night when it's too late to make a big dinner and we don't feel like going to a restaurant or ordering in. What we want to do is chill out in front of the television with a glass of wine and a satisfying snack. This simple one-bowl dish is just the thing. It's comfort food, and it only takes seconds to make using basics I always have on hand in my pantry. **PER 2–4 PERSONE**

2 cans (each 14 oz/398 mL) cannellini beans, drained and rinsed
1 stalk celery
1 can (6 oz/170 g) tuna, packed in oil or water, drained
Juice of half a lemon
1/2 cup (125 mL) extra-virgin olive oil
Salt and freshly ground pepper, QB

As with any canned legumes, give the beans a really good rinse under cold water in a strainer and wash off all the liquid. Transfer to a serving bowl. Chop up the celery and add it to the bowl along with the tuna. I prefer to use tuna packed in oil rather than in water. It tastes so much better. Just make sure you drain the oil very well. Add lemon juice, olive oil, and salt and pepper. *E buon appetito!*

INSALATA DI RISO
Rice Salad

Cold rice salad tastes better the longer it sits in the fridge. How can I be so sure? Well, when I was in my early 20s, I lived in Milan for a few months. My roommate and I, being on a very strict budget—in a word, poor—lived on huge bowls of insalata di riso. It was delicious, cheap and kept well in the fridge for several days.

You can make this dish with any type of rice you have on hand. I love serving it in the summer. Because it holds so well, it's a fantastic dish for a picnic. I often enjoy it as a simple meal in my garden, served with a glass of crisp white wine.

PER 4 PERSONE

1 cup (250 mL) rice
Fontina cheese, cubed, QB
1 large ball fresh mozzarella, cubed
Scamorza cheese, roughly chopped, QB
10 cherry tomatoes, quartered
1 cup (250 mL) black olives, pitted
3 tbsp (45 mL) capers, drained
5 anchovies, either roughly chopped or whole
1/4 cup (50 mL) extra-virgin olive oil
Salt, QB

Cook the rice according to package directions. Let it cool down in the fridge or run cold water over it, as I do. It must be cool before you make the salad.

Add the fontina, mozzarella and scamorza cheeses, cherry tomatoes, olives, capers, anchovies, olive oil and salt. Toss to combine. Then into the fridge it goes for at least 30 minutes or, better still, 1 hour, so that all those flavors have a chance to come together before serving.

Zuppe

Maybe it's because I grew up in Canada, but soups remind me of family, comfort and warmth. When winter comes, I find myself remembering my mom making pasta e fagioli. Or sometimes she made a stracciatella, starting with chicken broth or consommé and adding an egg beaten with grated Parmigiano to give it a fluffy texture.

Soups are about alchemy and about how nothing ever has to go to waste. In fact, some of Italy's most famous soups, like the classic Tuscan ribollita, are made to use up leftovers. Soups, perhaps more than any other food, can taste different every time you make them. They also taste better the longer they sit.

As a kid, I used to cringe when my mom would go through the reduced produce section. But what she would do in her kitchen with those less-than-perfect veggies was magical. And now I do the same thing. Most supermarkets discount vegetables that are about to go bad or are a bit too ripe or just don't look perfect. Don't buy the most pristine cauliflower or cabbage—buy the ones that are beaten up a bit and less expensive. Throw them in water with a handful of beans or lentils, some broken-up pasta, maybe a prosciutto bone and let everything simmer. Now you're talking alchemy!

The soups in this chapter have a real personality to them. Save money. Turn those rugged-looking characters into beauties. Teach your kids that food doesn't have to look pristine and beautiful. Teach them the art of transformation. It's *quanto basta*—use what you have and what you like, and don't be afraid to experiment.

NO STOCK? NO WORRIES

Don't feel that you need to have a freezer full of stock before you can even think about making soup. And don't even think about using a powdered soup base mix or a bouillon cube as a substitute. If you have either in your cupboard, stop reading now, get up and throw that stuff away. I promise you this book will still be here when you get back. They're full of salt, fat, MSG and flavor enhancers, and, more important, you simply don't need them. If you have pesto in the freezer, then you have your own flavor enhancer.

If you're boiling vegetables for dinner, or making a bollito—meat and vegetables cooked in water—then guess what? You've unintentionally made stock. Enjoy the meat for dinner, and use the cooking liquid as the base for a soup. As a super-quick fix, I often stop by my local butcher shop and buy the ends of the prosciutto, which they sell for a fraction of the price of the slices. I fry them up with some garlic or onions or both, pour in some water, and suddenly I have a flavorful base. Or, if you're really stuck, water is totally fine as a soup base. Don't sweat it.

BRODO
Stock

A stock is a flavorful liquid made of fish, meat and/or vegetables that have been simmered for a long time in water. The strained liquid is used as a flavor base for a number of dishes, from soups to risottos to stews. It can be made with inexpensive cuts of meat, bones, vegetables or vegetable trimmings and herbs. The more meat you use, the more flavor your stock will have.

This is where getting to know your butcher will really pay off. If you tell him you're making a stock, he'll almost do the prepping for you by giving you meaty soup bones or chicken parts that would otherwise be discarded. For fish stock, you can use fish bones and tails, as well as the heads, which are especially flavorful.

Basic Vegetables for Stock

These ingredients are the vegetable basics for all stocks on the following page:

2 carrots
1 onion (unpeeled), quartered
2 cloves garlic (unpeeled), smashed
1 stalk celery
1 bunch fresh flat-leaf parsley
4 or 5 whole black peppercorns
1 bay leaf
Whole fennel fronds (for the vegetable stock only)

The other common ingredient is water, of course. Pour in enough to cover the ingredients plus an extra 1 to 2 inches (2.5 to 5 cm).

I cook my stock without a lid, but if you use one, make sure it's only partially covering the pot so that the steam can escape. Remove the lid when letting the stock cool.

Don't stir the stock while it's cooking. There's no need to, and stirring will only make it cloudy. Just let it do its thing.

In the early stages of cooking a meat or fish stock, you'll see a scummy gray-brown foam rise to the top of the pot. You need to get rid of this. Simply skim off the foam with a wooden spoon and discard.

If you're making a chicken stock but don't plan to use it immediately, you can skip the foam skimming step above and let the stock cool in the fridge overnight. The fat will rise to the top and solidify, and you can just scoop or scrape it off.

Salt the stock at the end of cooking, not at the beginning. The liquid will cook down as it simmers, concentrating the flavor, and you don't want your brodo to be too salty.

For Meat or Fish Stock

Rinse the bones well and put them in a stockpot along with the basic vegetables and water. Bring to a gentle boil, then immediately lower the heat and simmer for 1 to 2 hours (or longer if you like), skimming off the foam occasionally. The longer the stock cooks, the more intense and flavorful it will be. Let it cool, uncovered. Strain out and discard the bones and vegetables. Cover and refrigerate the brodo for up to 5 days or freeze it for a few months.

For Chicken Stock

Rinse the chicken well and put it in a stockpot along with the basic vegetables and water. Bring to a gentle boil, then immediately lower the heat and simmer for 1 to 2 hours (or longer if you like), skimming off the foam occasionally. The longer the stock cooks, the more intense and flavorful it will be. Let it cool, uncovered. Remove the chicken and vegetables. Discard the vegetables. You can use the boiled chicken meat in your soup or in other recipes. Cover and refrigerate the brodo for up to 5 days or freeze it for a few months.

For Vegetable Stock

Put the basic vegetables, fennel fronds and water in a stockpot and bring to a boil. Immediately lower the heat and simmer for 1 to 2 hours. The longer the stock cooks, the more flavorful it will be. Let it cool, uncovered. Strain and discard the vegetables. Cover and refrigerate the brodo for up to 5 days or freeze it for a few months.

SOFFRITTO

A lot of Italian dishes start with a simple base called a *soffritto*. Once you learn to make it, you have the key to a world of soups, stews and sauces. A soffritto is generally made up of diced onions, carrots and celery, and sometimes garlic, and it's always done as the first step to create a flavor base for a variety of dishes.

Although the ingredients are basic, to me the size of the dice has an impact on the outcome. For instance, if I'm cooking something hearty like a meat or stew, I'll cut the vegetables slightly larger because I want the soffritto to maintain its presence in the finished dish. But for my soups, I'll use a fine dice—just enough that the soffritto has a subtle presence in a pappa al pomodoro or ribollita. For something like a bolognese sauce, in which I want the soffritto to add depth of flavor but not any texture, instead of trying to cut the vegetables into a superfine dice with my knife, I sometimes use a cheese grater to prepare them so that when I sauté them, they almost melt and become silky smooth.

The word *soffritto* means to "gently fry" or "sauté," and that's what you're going to do. Heat up a pan and pour in your extra-virgin olive oil. When the oil is hot, add the diced vegetables along with a little salt and pepper. Cook over medium-low heat for 15 to 20 minutes, stirring frequently to prevent sticking and burning, until the ingredients soften into each other.

If you don't believe how much flavor there is when these basic humble ingredients are cooked together, spread a little soffritto on a piece of bread and see for yourself!

ZUPPA DI PORCINI
Porcini Soup

This soup yields big return for little effort. Using fresh porcini mushrooms is essential. Porcini have such an intense aroma and flavor that you don't have to start off with onions or garlic—the mushrooms do all the work. The soup has an almost silky, delicate texture, yet it's meaty and flavorful enough to be comfort food. In Italy, you get a bunch of the herb nepitella with your porcini. It's a cross between mint and oregano, so if you can't get your hands on nepitella, a mix of fresh mint and oregano is fine. **PER 4 PERSONE**

4 large fresh porcini mushrooms
4 tbsp (60 mL) extra-virgin olive oil
2 tbsp (30 mL) unsalted butter
1 sprig nepitella, or a combination of equal parts fresh mint and oregano
5 cups (1.25 L) vegetable stock
Salt and freshly ground pepper, QB
2 eggs
1 cup (250 mL) freshly grated Parmigiano-Reggiano cheese

Clean the mushrooms by rubbing off any loose dirt with a clean dishtowel. With a paring knife, cut off any tough parts of the base or the root. Roughly chop the porcini.

Put your soup pot on medium-high heat and add the olive oil and butter. All the porcini go right into the pot. Stir them around. Once they've absorbed the oil and butter, add the herbs, a splash of the vegetable stock to prevent the porcini from sticking, and salt and pepper. The porcini will soften up and you'll have what looks like a thick sauce. Pour in enough of the remaining vegetable stock to cover the porcini. Bring to a boil, then lower the heat and let simmer, uncovered, for 20 to 30 minutes. In a small bowl, beat together the eggs and a good handful of Parmigiano. Drizzle that into the pot. Stir it and you'll see the egg break up and form into little silky strips. This helps thicken the soup. Serve immediately.

RIBOLLITA
Tuscan Leftover Soup

I never make my ribollita the same way twice. I don't feel bad about it because I'm honoring the origins of the dish. Ribollita is one of the recipes most associated with Tuscan cooking, and a perfect example of how economy and necessity come together in the Italian philosophy of making something new and better every day. Its origins are in *cucina povera*. The poor Tuscan farmer would have a pot of soup on the stove, and every day he'd add a little more water and a little bit of whatever was available to him. Hence the name *ribollita,* which means "to reboil." Ribollita is a very comforting dish. Some people like it soupy, but I prefer it thick enough that I can use a fork. I also like to eat it slightly warmer than room temperature, with a good drizzle of extra-virgin olive oil. **PER 6 PERSONE**

1 cup (250 mL) extra-virgin olive oil, plus extra for drizzling
1 clove garlic, finely chopped
1 onion, minced
1 carrot, minced
1 stalk celery, minced
1 or 2 small prosciutto rinds (optional)
1 potato, peeled and chopped
1/2 head savoy cabbage, thinly sliced
1/2 head cavolo nero or black cabbage, thinly sliced
Salt and freshly ground pepper, QB
2 cups (500 mL) cooked borlotti beans or 1 can (19 oz/540 mL) borlotti beans
2 cups (500 mL) tomato purée
4 cups (1 L) vegetable stock
6 slices Tuscan-style or dense country-style bread

Start with the soffritto: In a soup pot, heat the olive oil over medium heat. Add the garlic, onion, carrot, celery, and prosciutto rinds (if using). Sauté until the vegetables soften and the prosciutto rinds brown, then add the potatoes, savoy cabbage and cavolo nero, salt and pepper.

Once all the vegetables have wilted, add the borlotti beans. I like to mash up most of them with the back of the spoon, to thicken the soup and give it some texture, but don't you dare make this perfect! You want it to be rustic and uneven. For me, the more texture, the more taste.

Add the tomato purée, stock and bread. Some recipes suggest that you leave the bread out of this step and instead put a slice in each serving bowl and pour the soup over it. But I prefer to add the bread to the soup at this point and stir it every so often so the bread softens, breaks up and creates that nice thick *pappa* consistency that ribollita is known for. When it's finished cooking, I always let it sit for about an hour off the heat so the flavors can really come together. Serve it with a good drizzle of extra-virgin olive oil.

ZUPPA DI ZUCCA
Squash Soup

I love butternut squash. It's one of my favorite vegetables. It has a silky, sweet taste, and it doesn't take much to make it into an incredibly satisfying, comforting soup. **PER 4 PERSONE**

4 tbsp (60 mL) butter
1 potato, cubed
1 1/4 lb (625 g) butternut squash, peeled, seeded and cubed
Salt and freshly ground pepper, QB
3 cups (750 mL) vegetable stock
1/2 cup (125 mL) whipping cream (35%)
Freshly grated Parmigiano-Reggiano cheese, QB
Truffle oil, for drizzling (optional)

Melt the butter in a pot over medium-high heat. You can also use olive oil if you prefer; it works just as well. Add the potatoes, squash, and salt and pepper. The smaller the vegetable cubes, the faster they cook. At this point, you're sautéing to caramelize them slightly and get the flavors going. When they're slightly brown, pour in a couple of ladlefuls of vegetable stock or as much as needed to cover the vegetables. Turn down the heat to medium and cook until the vegetables are fork-tender, about 10 minutes.

Now pour the mixture into a blender and blend, in batches if necessary, until it reaches a silky, even consistency. (You can also use a hand blender directly in the pot.) Pour it back into the pot and add the cream and Parmigiano. Cook over low heat for a few more minutes so the flavors can develop. Ladle into soup bowls. For a special treat, finish each portion with a drizzle of truffle oil.

Un' altra idea: This also makes a fantastic sauce for a grilled chicken breast, or for roast turkey, beef or pork. After sautéing the squash and potatoes, add a little vegetable stock just enough so they don't stick to the pan and cook until soft. Add some Gorgonzola cheese and let it melt.

ZUPPA DI VONGOLE
Clam Soup

A few years ago, in the Neapolitan port town of Pozzuoli, I met a fisherman, Gennaro, and his wife, Maria, who ran a little hole-in-the-wall restaurant. They made some of the best fish soups I've ever had. Gennaro would tease me that his zuppa di vongole had a secret ingredient. One day, he took me back to the kitchen, where Maria was just beginning to make the soup, and he let me in on their secret. They put a small stone from the sea in the pan when sautéing the garlic in olive oil. He told me it adds loads of flavor. I don't know if it was the stone, but their zuppa was incredible. Since then, I've made this several times, and even without a stone, it seems to turn out pretty well! And whenever I prepare it, I think of Gennaro and Maria.

2 lb (1 kg) fresh clams

1/4 cup (50 mL) extra-virgin olive oil, plus extra for drizzling

3 cloves garlic (2 finely chopped, 1 for rubbing)

1 fresh chili pepper, diced, or dried chili pepper, crushed, QB (optional)

1 stone from the sea (optional)

10 cherry tomatoes, quartered (optional)

1 cup (250 mL) white wine

Salt, QB

1 bunch fresh flat-leaf parsley, finely chopped

4 slices Tuscan-style or dense country-style bread, toasted and halved

The clams are very easy to clean and prepare. Put them in a bowl of fresh cold water, add salt and let them sit for about 30 minutes. The salted water simulates the sea, and the clams will open up and release any sand and grit, then close. Drain and rinse them.

Heat up a large soup pot over medium heat and pour in the olive oil. Add the finely chopped garlic and diced chili pepper. I love chili peppers, because they add a wonderful color and, of course, a hearty kick, but you can leave them out or adjust the amount depending on how hot you want your dish. If you're using a sea stone, drop it in the pot. Next, a few pomodorini—cherry tomatoes. Again, these are optional, but they add wonderful flavor and color. Cook everything for a few minutes or until the tomatoes begin to soften and lose their shape.

Add the clams and cover with the lid. Shake the pan a few times to help stimulate the clams to open. It's important that they steam in all the flavors of the garlic and the olive oil (and the stone, according to Gennaro and Maria). The clams release some water, which is the base for the soup. Add a generous splash of white wine and a little bit of salt. Put the lid back on and let the whole thing simmer for 2 to 4 minutes or until the clams open up. Now, depending on your mood, you can make this more soupy by adding a little more wine or even a few spoonfuls of tomato purée. Finish by sprinkling some parsley over the soup. Don't forget to remove the stone!

Serve along with toasted country-style bread rubbed with garlic and drizzled with olive oil.

PER 4 PERSONE

Un' altra idea: If you want to use mussels instead of clams, go for it, or try mixing the two.

Un idea per la pasta: This recipe is in the Zuppe section because it's one of my favorite soups, but it's also one of my favorite pasta sauces—a.k.a. Spaghetti alla Vongole. When your spaghetti is perfectly al dente, drain the pasta really well and add it to the clam mixture. Cook over medium to high heat so that the starches come out and the broth reduces, thickening and coating the pasta.

Salse

talians aren't big on heavy or fancy sauces. In Italian cooking, the sauce isn't made to drown out the flavors or cover up poor-quality ingredients, but rather to enhance or complement ingredients. Some sauces are meant to show off an ingredient. Pesto, for instance, offers a chance to use up basil when it's plentiful in the garden. As you'll see, it sometimes takes only five minutes to bring a few ingredients together and make magic.

SALSA DI CINQUE MINUTI DI MIA MAMMA
My Mother's Five-Minute Tomato Sauce

When I was a kid, my mom used to ask us whether we wanted pasta with her *salsa di cinque minuti*, her magic five-minute sauce. She called it that because it literally took five minutes to make.

Fast-forward to my college days and hanging out with my buddies. When it came to suppertime, there would be the Big Debate: should we order in? I'd say, "Guys, we can have an amazing plate of pasta with my mother's tomato sauce and be done in the time it would take for your food to get here." I was always teased about being a mamma's boy. But after dinner, they always wanted the recipe.

So here's my mother's sauce. You can use store-bought canned tomatoes; don't feel guilty for using a canned or jarred product. Tomato season is short, and the ones that end up in cans are picked at their peak and are flavorful. In fact, I think that canned tomatoes should be a staple in your pantry. For this sauce, make sure there's nothing in the can but tomatoes—no added salt, sugar or basil.

MAKES ABOUT 4 CUPS (1 L), ENOUGH FOR 4 SERVINGS OF PASTA.

4 tbsp (60 mL) extra-virgin olive oil
2 cloves garlic, coarsely chopped
Chili pepper flakes, QB (optional)
1 can (28 oz/796 mL) tomato purée or plum tomatoes
Salt, QB
5 fresh basil leaves

Heat up your olive oil and brown the garlic and, if you like a bit of heat, some chili pepper flakes. You can substitute onions for the garlic or use both, depending on what you like. When they're gently browned, throw in your tomato purée and some salt and let it simmer for 5 minutes. Tear up some fresh basil and toss it in, and there you have it.

Un' altra idea: For a different texture, you can use peeled plum tomatoes. Put them in a bowl and squeeze them with your hands until they're the texture you want. Or add a bit of whipping cream to the tomato sauce to make a rosé sauce. And the good news is you can probably make this in the time it takes you to read this page.

SALSA VERDE

In Florence, all over *il centro*, you'll find little porchetta and bollito stands that sell panini on which the owner drizzles salsa verde. The locals pick their favorite stand according to the quality of the sauce, because that's what elevates the sandwich.

This simple cold sauce is a Tuscan classic that was created to be served alongside boiled meats, but it's also great on sandwiches with cheese, prosciutto or salami. I like to use it as a healthier and tastier substitute for mayo. It adds incredible flavor and holds really well in the fridge. It's also perfect on warm or cold roasted meats, chicken or even fish. The recipe calls for basic ingredients, but you can alter the quantities to taste.   **MAKES 2 CUPS (500 ML)**

1 large bunch fresh flat-leaf parsley, leaves only
3 or 4 fresh basil leaves
3 or 4 cloves garlic
4 anchovies
4 tbsp (60 mL) capers, drained
1 1/2 cups (375 mL) extra-virgin olive oil

Using a mezzaluna and cutting board, coarsely chop the parsley, basil and garlic until they're about half chopped. Add the anchovies and capers to the cutting board and continue chopping until everything is evenly minced. Transfer the mixture to a jar and add the olive oil, mixing until it's a thick, luscious green sauce. Taste and add more salt if necessary; because of the anchovies, it might be just right as is.

Un' altra idea: For Salsa Verde that's ideal for grilled fish, especially calamari, add 2 tbsp (30 mL) freshly squeezed lemon juice.

SALSA BESCIAMELLA
Béchamel Sauce

So, you're probably asking yourself, what's a French sauce doing in a cookbook by a proud Italian boy? Well, the answer is that a version of besciamella originated in Italy during the Roman era. In the 1400s, Catherine de Medici married into the French royal family, ultimately becoming queen, and brought her Italian chef with her to France. And the rest, as they say, is history.

A good béchamel sauce can add that *je ne sais quoi* to many of your pasta, meat or vegetable recipes. But for me, there's nothing like a beautiful layered lasagna with a great meat sauce and little pockets of creamy besciamella. You might think that this sauce is tricky to make. But it's actually just a matter of keeping your eye on it and knowing what to look out for.

MAKES APPROXIMATELY 4 CUPS (1 L), ENOUGH FOR 1 LASAGNA

4 tbsp (60 mL) butter
4 cups (1 L) milk
4 tbsp (60 mL) all-purpose flour

Get out 2 pots and place them over medium heat. In one pot, melt the butter; in the other, warm up the milk. Be careful not to brown the butter. Once it's melted, remove it from the heat and start whisking in your flour a little at a time. Keep going until it's all incorporated. At this point, I'd bet money that your mixture is going to ball up and get lumpy, and maybe even a little gluey. That's okay—don't freak out.

Now, over to the second pot. Just before the milk reaches the boiling point, remove it from the heat. Add a few ladlefuls to the pot with the flour and butter. Put the flour mixture back on the burner and start whisking. When the milk is absorbed, add some more, a little at a time and stir, stir, stir until you've used up all the milk. Keep whisking until your sauce reaches a creamy, velvety consistency.

PESTO

In the late '80s, pesto became the "it" sauce. It seemed as if every pizza shop that wanted to be a bit more upscale or even gourmet did it by creating its own pesto pizza. Well, I can tell you this: there's nothing gourmet about pesto. It's as homey, simple and rustic as it gets. In fact, it's one of the easiest sauces to make because it truly uses the QB philosophy. All cooks have their own variation. Although pesto requires just a basic list of ingredients, no two are the same because you can adjust to suit your taste.

When I was growing up, pesto was a staple in the fridge and freezer. When basil was in season, my mom would make a big batch and store it in the freezer. I still do that now. And pesto was also my mother's secret flavor enhancer. I call it Italian MSG. I throw a tablespoonful into soups. A spoonful would also put a new spin on a simple tomato sauce or even a zuppa di pesce.

Among Italian cooks, you'll find many different techniques for making pesto. Some people like to do it in a food processor; others say that technique crushes the leaves and takes away some of the flavor. In Genoa, where the sauce was invented, most cooks insist that the only way to make pesto is to use a mortar and pestle, which grinds the basil, thereby ensuring the oils are properly released and incorporated into the other ingredients. Other people prefer to make it on a board with a mezzaluna.

No matter what the method, everyone agrees on these key ingredients: basil that's in season, fresh garlic, the best-quality pine nuts and extra-virgin olive oil. I'm going to give you my favorite techniques, but no matter how you choose to make it, there are some musts.

1. First, make sure your basil leaves are completely dry. Water will make your pesto turn brown and spoil sooner. Wash the basil well, then spin it in a salad spinner to get all the water out, and pat dry with a cloth. I prefer to use Genovese basil, which has smaller leaves and, I think, a sweeter taste.

2. Garlic? Well, definitely QB. I know that people get a little crazy when it comes to Italian cooking and think that garlic makes it authentic. But it is raw garlic, so you have to be careful. Too much and you're in danger of overpowering everything with a bitter garlic aftertaste. That's not a great thing, in my opinion, in a sauce that's made to take advantage of lovely sweet basil.

3. I like to use coarse sea salt. The texture of the salt actually helps grind the leaves, to get all the great fragrance and oils out of the basil.

4. Oh yeah, about the pine nuts: I like to lightly toast them. This isn't necessary, and true Geno-vese pesto does not call for it, but I like the nutty flavor brought out by toasting. It takes only a few minutes. Throw them into a dry frying pan on low heat and keep your eye on them, because they're delicate and can burn very quickly.

5. Last thing: Parmigiano-Reggiano. Make sure you always buy fresh Parmigiano. Don't buy the pre-grated stuff. You don't know what you're getting.

4 cups (1 L) fresh basil leaves, washed and thoroughly dried
1/2 cup (125 mL) pine nuts, toasted
2 cloves garlic
1 1/2 tsp (7 mL) coarse sea salt
1 cup (250 mL) extra-virgin olive oil
1 cup (250 mL) freshly grated Parmigiano-Reggiano cheese

Put your basil, pine nuts, garlic and salt in your mortar and, with the pestle, begin to press and mulch all the ingredients into a paste. Slowly drizzle in some olive oil until it's the texture you like. Now add your Parmigiano to the mortar and mix until it's thoroughly combined and there's an even consistency.

To keep your pesto from spoiling, make sure you top up your jar with extra-virgin olive oil and store it in the fridge.

Although I'm a mortar and pestle guy, I have also made pesto with a mezzaluna, and it's pretty neat. You put the basil, pine nuts and garlic on a wooden cutting board, then rock your mezza-luna back and forth over everything, finely chopping it into a paste. When done, put it in a jar, add some salt, extra-virgin olive oil and Parmigiano and stir really well. Make sure you top it off with more oil to help preserve the pesto.

MAKES 2 TO 3 CUPS (500 TO 750 ML)

Pesto Amalfitano: There are many versions of pesto. This one has been made along the Amalfi coast for, oh, about 700 years, give or take. Essentially, you substitute parsley for the basil and walnuts for the pine nuts. It's a little sharper and less sweet than the basil pesto, but good. You can use it with fresh pasta or grilled fish. And I'd definitely recommend using it as a seasoning in soups and stews.

SALSA DI PORCINI
Porcini Sauce

Porcini mushrooms have a meaty texture, and yet are soft and flavorful, which makes this sauce extremely versatile. It works well on toasted crostini, and is delicious on meat or poultry. In fact, if you think of this as a topping more than a sauce, you'll find lots of uses for it.

This calls for fresh porcini mushrooms, but it also works well with mixed mushrooms. So if porcini aren't in season or not available, you can substitute oyster or button mushrooms, or, better yet, a mix of both. Although dried porcini are available year-round, I don't recommend them for this recipe. They're better for risottos. When you buy porcini mushrooms in Tuscany, the vendor gives you a little bouquet of a wild herb called nepitella, which tastes like a cross between mint and oregano. So if you can't get nepitella but want to get a sense of that Tuscan flavor, substitute equal parts fresh mint and oregano. Or you can use flat-leaf parsley. All work well, and each herb adds something slightly different to the dish.

PER 4 PERSONE

4 fresh porcini mushrooms
2 sprigs nepitella, or a combination of equal parts fresh mint and oregano, or fresh flat-leaf parsley, QB
4 tbsp (60 mL) extra-virgin olive oil, plus extra for drizzling
2 cloves garlic, finely chopped
Salt and freshly ground pepper, QB
8 slices Tuscan-style or dense country-style bread

With a dry dish towel, brush off any dirt that may be on the porcini mushrooms (do not rinse them under water, as they will absorb it like a sponge). Use a knife to scrape off any remaining dirt and to peel back the top layer of skin if they're really dirty. Give the mushrooms an uneven rough chop. And chop your herbs.

In a pan, heat up the olive oil over medium heat and add the garlic. After you've got that going for about 20 or 30 seconds, add your porcini mushrooms and sauté for about 5 minutes or until they release some of their liquid and the liquid evaporates. Add the herbs, salt and pepper. If you're serving this on crostini, toast or grill your bread, then spoon the porcini sauce on top, with a drizzle of olive oil as the final touch.

Un' altra idea: If you like, at the very end, just before the porcini are done, add 2 tbsp (30 mL) heavy cream (35%). Sauté over high heat and let the cream reduce, and you'll have a porcini mushroom cream sauce to die for.

SALSA DI TONNO E CREMA
Tuna and Cream Sauce

I like to think I invented this sauce when I was ten. I discovered what a little bit of heavy cream can do when reduced in a sauce. I was experimenting with my mother's Salsa di Cinque Minuti at the time. Of course, this sauce existed before me, but that didn't take away from the joy of creation. And it shows you two things: how you can add ingredients to a good basic recipe to suit your own taste and create your own version, like a true alchemist; and that, if you teach your kids some simple techniques in the kitchen, before long they'll be writing cookbooks about you! Okay, I have a challenge for you. The next time someone in your family wants to order pizza, make a bet with them. They order a pizza, and you make this pasta. See which one is ready first—and which tastes better. **PER 4 PERSONE**

1 lb (500 g) penne, fusilli or any other short pasta
12 black olives
8 large sun-dried tomatoes, chopped
4 tbsp (60 mL) extra-virgin olive oil,
    plus extra for drizzling
1 clove garlic, finely chopped
2 cups (500 mL) tomato purée or tomato sauce (see page 171)
1 can (7 oz/198 g) tuna, packed in oil
1/2 cup (125 mL) whipping cream (35%)
1 bunch fresh flat-leaf parsley, finely chopped
Salt, QB

Cook your pasta until al dente. While it's cooking, make the sauce: Pit the olives by pressing down on them with the side of your chef's knife. The olives will open up and you'll be able to pick out the pits. Give both the olives and sun-dried tomatoes a rough chop.

Heat the olive oil in a pan, then gently brown the garlic, olives and sun-dried tomatoes. Add the tomato purée or sauce and cook for 5 minutes. Then in go your tuna and whipping cream. Let this simmer for a few minutes, and it's ready. Taste it and see if it needs salt.

Drain your pasta, reserving 1/2 cup (125 mL) or so of the cooking water. Add the pasta to the pan of sauce, and pour in a bit of the reserved cooking water to help bind everything together. Cook for a minute or so on high heat. Take a moment to note that the pizza has not yet arrived, but the house smells great, and you sure feel bad for those waiting for the pizza. At this point, you may want to add another 1/2 cup (125 mL) of cream. Just make sure you cook the pasta long enough to let the cream reduce and thicken up the sauce. Either way, when everything is cooking together, add the finely chopped parsley and salt and mix well.

SALSA BOLOGNESE
Bolognese Meat Sauce

Salsa bolognese is one of those classic sauces associated with Italian cuisine. It's a rich, meat-based ragù that comes from the Emilia-Romagna region. As with most Italian classics, there are always going to be slight variations, little touches from region to region and from cook to cook that make each version special. No one can claim that theirs is the definitive version, so I won't pretend that the recipe below is the only way this sauce should be done. But I can promise that it's easy and tastes amazing. This is a great sauce to make on a weekend, when it can simmer away and perfume the house.

Salsa bolognese reminds me of Sunday afternoons at the Roccos', when my mom would have the sauce simmering, my cousins would come over, and the house would be alive with family and the anticipation of the *pranzo*. This is one of my favorite sauces, and it works with any type of fresh or dried pasta or gnocchi.   PER 6–8 PERSONE

1 onion, finely chopped
1 stalk celery, finely chopped
1 large carrot, peeled and finely chopped
3 tbsp (45 mL) extra-virgin olive oil
2 tbsp (30 mL) unsalted butter
1/2 lb (250 g) ground beef
1/2 lb (250 g) ground pork

1 cup (250 mL) white wine
1 cup (250 mL) milk
3 cups (750 mL) tomato purée
Salt, QB
5 fresh basil leaves

Note: If you re using the bolognese sauce for lasagna, increase the tomato purée to 5 cups (1.25 L) and add 1 cup (250 mL) water.

Start by making your classic soffritto (see page 153). I would encourage you to chop your onion, celery and carrot as finely as possible or do what I usually do: use a cheese grater to grate the vegetables, so they almost melt when you sauté them. Heat up a pan and add the olive oil and the soffritto mixture, taking time to gently brown your vegetables so the flavors become sweet and intense.

At this point, add the butter along with the ground beef and pork. Cook over medium to high heat until the meat is browned. Stir in the wine and cook until it's evaporated. Add the milk, which will give a slightly creamy texture and soften the meat as well. Add the tomato purée and salt, and simmer over low heat for a few hours, stirring occasionally. When the sauce is finished, tear up some basil leaves to add to it.

Primi

Primo in Italian means "first." This is the course you have right after your antipasto. It usually consists of a starch, like pasta or risotto, or, in the north, polenta. During a traditional Italian meal, *il primo* is served on its own, not with a side or a vegetable.

I can assure you that the low-carb diet never had a chance in Italy. I don't know why carbs have gotten such a bad rap. It's not the starch that makes a pasta fattening and heavy, but what you put on it.

I love my carbs! Growing up, I had to have one pasta or risotto a day. There's nothing better to me than well-cooked pasta with a simple sauce.

PASTA BASICS

As simple as pasta is to cook, there are certain things you need to know.

First, there's the issue of what to put in the cooking water with the pasta. When the water comes to a boil, salt it liberally. That gives the pasta flavor. There's a myth that says you should add a little oil to the boiling water to prevent the pasta from sticking. In Italy, they'd throw you in jail for that! Add your pasta to the boiling salted water, give it a stir, then stir a few more times in the first 20 or 30 seconds, and it won't stick. I promise.

Then there's the issue of how long to cook the pasta to achieve the right al dente texture for your own taste. Al dente pasta is soft on the outside and slightly firm, or slightly raw, in the middle. You want the pasta to have a bit of bite left in it so that when you mix it with the sauce it will still have some starchiness and firmness to help the sauce bind to it. It's not limp—it actually has some fight in it. It's not mushy like baby food. You have to do some work to eat it. There's texture. Sometimes I'm criticized for leaving my pasta a little too firm, too al dente, but that's *my* taste! In fact, I have a buddy in Naples who likes his spaghetti *molto* al dente, as do I. Whenever we go to a restaurant, we tell the waiter that we want our spaghetti cooked so that it barely has enough flex to wrap around the fork! Maybe that's a bit of an exaggeration, but you get the idea.

So cook your pasta to just before the al dente stage and drain it, reserving some of the cooking liquid, about 1/2 to 1 cup (125 to 250 mL). Then add the cooked pasta to the pan with the sauce and cook for a minute on high heat using a bit of the pasta water, as needed, to bind the sauce. The pasta will finish cooking to the al dente stage, and you'll see alchemy as it starts to glisten when the starch releases and the sauce sticks to the pasta.

And finally, it's not just about having a good *sugo,* or sauce; it's about matching the sauce to the shape of the pasta. Even though all pastas are essentially the same recipe—flour, water and, in the case of fresh pasta, sometimes egg—the shape has a real effect on how a dish actually tastes. Should your sugo go with a penne regate or penne lisce? Then there's the wider rigatoni. I prefer spaghetti over linguine because I like the texture, but I'd never use spaghetti for a matriciana sauce. For me, it has to be bucatini. And so on.

SPAGHETTI CON POMODORINI E PECORINO
Spaghetti with Cherry Tomatoes and Pecorino

There are few things that give me more pleasure than going into the garden, picking a handful of sweet pomodorini, or cherry tomatoes, and turning them into a fresh, light, simple tomato sauce. To me, that says summer. This is a version of the Salsa di Cinque Minuti di Mia Mamma that I call my two-minute sauce. It's a delicate sauce that's more about assembly than cooking. But in summer, when tomatoes are fresh from the vine and full of flavor, this is heaven. **PER 4 PERSONE**

1 lb (500 g) spaghetti
25 cherry tomatoes
4 tbsp (60 mL) extra-virgin olive oil, plus extra for drizzling
3 cloves garlic, finely chopped
Salt, QB
Fresh basil leaves, QB
Freshly grated pecorino cheese, QB

Heat up a pot of water to cook the pasta. While it's cooking, cut your cherry tomatoes in half.

Heat a pan over medium-high heat and add the olive oil and garlic. Gently sauté for about a minute, then add the pomodorini and salt. Now, depending on how you want the texture, you can either gently sauté the tomatoes so that they lose a bit of their shape but are still identifiable, or you can keep going until they melt into each other and look more like a sauce. I've done it both ways, and both work well. It depends on your mood.

Once the pasta is done to the pre–al dente stage, reserve about 1/2 cup (125 mL) of the cooking water, drain your pasta and put it right into the pan with the sauce. Mix it together, adding some of the pasta water to help bind everything together. And now rip up some basil leaves to throw in and grate your cheese over the pasta. You could use Parmigiano, but for this recipe I prefer a hard pecorino. It's salty and a bit sharper, and perfectly balances the sweetness of the cherry tomatoes.

Plate the pasta, and finish it off with a drizzle of very good extra-virgin olive oil.

PASTA MARE E MONTI DI PEPPE
Peppe's Surf and Turf Pasta

Mio caro amico Peppe runs a restaurant on the beautiful island of Ischia. He calls it Aglio, Olio e Pomodoro, which translates as the much less romantic-sounding Garlic, Oil and Tomatoes.

I'll tell you the truth: Peppe has my dream job. He runs this little restaurant with his wife. It's on the beach. He has no set menu and cooks whatever he feels like. If you go there, you'll see him running the kitchen on his own, hanging out in his flip-flops and shorts, cooking because he loves it. When I grow up, I want to be just like Peppe. In the meantime, I content myself with making this brilliantly simple but fantastic pasta.

1 lb (500 g) paccheri or rigatoni pasta
5 tbsp (75 mL) extra-virgin olive oil
2 cloves garlic, chopped
1 tsp (5 mL) chili pepper flakes (optional)
2 small zucchini, thinly sliced
12 cherry tomatoes, halved
16 large shrimp or scampi
Salt, QB
1 1/2 cups (375 mL) white wine
Freshly grated Parmigiano-Reggiano cheese, for sprinkling
1 bunch fresh flat-leaf parsley, chopped

Cook your pasta. By the time it's done, your sauce will be ready.

Pour the olive oil into a pan heated over medium-high heat. Then in go the garlic, chili pepper flakes and zucchini. Sauté for a minute, keeping an eye on it to make sure the zucchini doesn't burn. Add the cherry tomatoes and shrimp (deveining is optional) and cook for a few minutes longer. Add some salt and the wine. Let the wine reduce.

There's a bit of a dance here, because you don't want soupy pasta, but you also don't want to overcook the shrimp or the zucchini. So if they're done before the sauce has reduced, remove them and let the liquid thicken up.

When the sauce has thickened, throw in your pasta, add some grated Parmigiano and sprinkle in some parsley. If you've taken anything out, put it back in. Give it a couple of tosses over high heat to encourage the flavors to mingle. And you're done.

Note: If you love seafood and aren't squeamish, keep the heads on the shrimp or scampi. Then when you're eating them, rip the heads off and suck out all that awesome flavor. Don't be shy about eating shrimp that way, even if you're at a restaurant. Any good chef would be proud to see you do so!

PER 4 PERSONE

Un' altra idea: Substitute porcini mushrooms for the zucchini and 1/2 cup (125 mL) whipping cream (35%) for the Parmigiano. Porcini mushrooms and shrimp are heavenly together. I'd also recommend using fettuccine instead of paccheri.

When I was in Sicily, I was in heaven—pasta heaven, that is. To me, anything with fried eggplant, ricotta salata and pasta is, well, *da Dio!* Everyone in Sicily makes Pasta alla Norma, with subtle variations, of course, but no one I met on my travels there can tell you who Norma is.

PASTA ALLA NORMA
Norma's Pasta

For me, perfect pasta alla Norma is about making sure the eggplant is fried to a crisp, deep golden brown. Make sure the olive oil is hot. If it's not hot enough, the eggplant will absorb the oil like a sponge, and it will end up soggy and oily instead of crispy. The second most important thing is to use a semi-soft ricotta salata. This is ricotta that starts off soft, but each day salt is added to the top to drain out the water, until the cheese becomes semi-hard, salty and slightly sharp. If you can't find ricotta salata, a sharp-tasting pecorino cheese will also work. **PER 4 PERSONE**

4 tbsp (60 mL) extra-virgin olive oil, plus extra for frying eggplant
1/2 white onion, chopped
1 can (14 oz/398 mL) plum tomatoes
Salt and freshly ground pepper, QB
1 medium eggplant, cubed
1 lb (500 g) penne rigate pasta
Fresh basil leaves, torn, QB
Freshly grated ricotta salata cheese, for sprinkling

Heat your pan over medium-high heat and add the olive oil. Put in the onions and gently sauté until they're lightly golden. Add the tomatoes. I like to use plum tomatoes because I don't want a perfectly smooth sauce; I like to see little bits of tomato. But if all you have on hand is a purée, that's perfectly fine. With the back of a wooden spoon, break up the plum tomatoes into little chunks. Add salt and pepper and cook until the sauce is thickened.

In another pan over high heat, heat up about 1 inch (2.5 cm) of olive oil until it's very hot but not smoking. Be careful, as olive oil burns more quickly than vegetable oil, but to me there's no substitute. Fry the eggplant until golden and drain on a paper towel to absorb the excess oil. While the eggplant is draining, cook your pasta. Drain the pasta just before the al dente stage and add it to the tomato sauce. The pasta will finish cooking in the sauce. Add the fried eggplant and basil leaves. Sprinkle with some of the ricotta salata. Mix so the pasta and sauce are really well combined. Plate, sprinkle extra ricotta salata on top and serve immediately.

Un' altra idea: Add some mozzarella and, if you like, some scamorza cheese and spoon it into a baking dish. Throw it into a 400°F (200°C) oven for about 20 minutes or until golden. Now you have Norma al forno!

GNUDI
Naked Ravioli

By now, you're probably tired of hearing me say this, but this is one of the easiest recipes you'll ever make, and the results are mind-blowing. It takes only about five minutes to make, yet it's elegant enough for a dinner party. Gnudi is naked ravioli, or ravioli without the pasta. But that description doesn't do it justice. These will melt in your mouth. **PER 4 PERSONE**

1 lb (500 g) fresh ricotta cheese,
  preferably sheep's milk, drained
1 large bunch raw spinach, chopped
5 tbsp (75 mL) extra-virgin olive oil,
  plus extra for smearing hands
4 cloves garlic, finely chopped

Salt, QB
4 tbsp (60 mL) freshly grated Parmigiano-Reggiano
  cheese, plus extra for sprinkling
All-purpose flour
20 cherry tomatoes, halved
4 to 8 fresh basil leaves, chopped

Place your drained ricotta in a mixing bowl. Chop your spinach and sauté it with some olive oil and garlic. Let it cool down, then add it to the ricotta. Add 2 pinches of salt, a good handful of Parmigiano and mix it up. Feel free to adjust the quantities to suit your taste. If you like more Parmigiano, or more spinach, by all means add more! You can taste the mixture at this point to make sure it's just right for you. If the texture seems a bit liquid to you, add a pinch of flour, but not too much. You just want to bind the mixture. The texture should be fluffy and delicate, not heavy.

Now comes the fun part. Pour a bit of olive oil on your hands and rub them together. This will prevent the gnudi mixture from sticking to your hands, and the bonus is that your hands get a nice spa treatment at the same time. Now, take a bit of the mixture and roll it in your hands to make little balls about the size of golf balls. Keep going until you've used up all the ricotta mixture.

For the tomato sauce: You can use the Salsa di Cinque Minuti di Mia Mamma (page 171). Or make this sauce: Cut up some cherry tomatoes. Heat some olive oil and garlic in a pan, throw in the tomatoes along with some salt and cook for a few minutes until they get soft.

Spread a layer of tomato sauce in a baking dish. Lay the gnudi on top, then spoon some more of the sauce on top. Sprinkle some Parmigiano on top of each gnudi ball. Toss the basil on top. Bake the whole thing in a 350° to 400°F (180° to 200°C) oven for 10 to 15 minutes or until golden. For a nice presentation, you can also bake these in individual dishes.

Un' altra idea: Use your gnudi to fill ravioli, cannelloni or any other shell pasta. Cook your favorite type of dried pasta shell in boiling water for a minute or so, just enough to soften slightly. Drain them, run under cold water so you can handle them easily, and fill them with the gnudi mixture. Lay the filled shells in a baking dish and pour some tomato sauce and 1/2 cup (125 mL) water over them. Sprinkle some grated Parmigiano-Reggiano over top and bake in a 350°F (180°C) oven for about 20 minutes.

PASTA AL FORNO
Oven-Baked Pasta

I've always wondered why pasta al forno never earned the same iconic status as lasagna. Now, don't get me wrong—I love lasagna. But pasta al forno is just as good and, in fact, sometimes even better, because it takes half the time to make and you simply can't mess it up. I promise you. I've given this recipe to friends who couldn't boil water, and it has become legendary in their home.

Now, for those of you who have never had this dish, let me describe it. When it comes out of the oven, the top will be nice and golden, and the edges and corners beautifully crispy and crunchy. At our Sunday *pranzo*, when my mom would bring it to the table, we kids would fight for the corners because those crunchy bits are so good! Of course, being my mom's favorite, I would win. Then again, there were four corners and three kids—four, if you count my dad. Underneath all of that beautiful crunchiness is a soft pasta infused with the sauce, the eggplant and olives, and those beautiful cheeses. Just serving it with the cheeses oozing out will make everyone salivate. The key to this dish is the cheese. You can choose your favorite combination, but I highly recommend using scamorza because the smokiness gives extra flavor.

I'm often asked what I'd pick for my last meal. The menu is as follows: a great burger, lasagna and, for dessert, pasta al forno.

1 lb (500 g) rigatoni pasta
4 tbsp (60 mL) extra-virgin olive oil
2 cloves garlic, chopped
1 large eggplant, cubed
15 infornate olives or any black olives, pitted and chopped
10 large sun-dried tomatoes, chopped
2 dried chili peppers, crushed (optional)
Salt, QB
3 cups (750 mL) tomato purée
3/4 lb (375 g) mozzarella cheese, shredded
Smoked scamorza cheese, roughly chopped
Freshly grated Parmigiano-Reggiano cheese, for sprinkling

Usually I'd tell you to cook your pasta al dente. For this dish, don't worry about it. Because it's going to be baked, it doesn't matter if the pasta is overcooked. So boil the water and cook your pasta.

Now for the sauce: Heat up a saucepan over medium-high heat. Pour in the extra-virgin olive oil and brown up the garlic. Make sure the oil is hot before adding the eggplant, olives, sun-dried tomatoes and chili peppers. Sauté the whole thing until the eggplant gets soft and is slightly golden. If you need to add a bit more oil, go easy. Eggplant absorbs oil like crazy, so you don't want to overdo it or you'll weigh down the dish and feel like you've eaten a brick. When the eggplant is nice and golden, add some salt and the tomato purée. Simmer for 5 to 10 minutes or until the pasta is ready.

Drain the pasta and return it to the pot. Add all the sauce, and the mozzarella and scamorza cheeses. Stir really well. Pour the whole thing into a large baking dish. Top with a good sprinkle of Parmigiano and bake in a 400°F (200°C) oven for about 30 minutes or until beautifully golden and crisp.

PER 4–6 PERSONE

CACIO E PEPE
Cheese and Cracked Pepper Pasta

You'll find this simple but satisfying dish on the menu in many trattorias in Rome. It's also a staple at my house. As with so many Italian dishes, there are different spins on it. Some call for olive oil, some for a little bit of cream. But for me, this dish is all about the simplicity of three ingredients: freshly ground pepper, pecorino romano cheese and a good egg pasta.

For this dish, I prefer to use a fresh egg noodle called tonnarelli, sometimes also called maccheroni alla chitarra. It's a long pasta cut on a special device with wire strings—it resembles a guitar. The unique design makes each noodle square. If you can't find this type of pasta, you can use spaghetti or, as they sometimes do in Rome, bucatini. Whatever pasta you choose, I recommend that it be fresh, not dried, for this recipe, because you want the more delicate flavor and texture that only a beautifully made fresh pasta can deliver.

I urge you to find a good *pastificio*, or fresh pasta shop, in your neighborhood. Although making fresh pasta is not hard, it can be time-consuming.

PER 4 PERSONE

1 lb (500 g) fresh egg pasta
2 tbsp (30 mL) black peppercorns
2 cups (500 mL) freshly grated pecorino cheese

Fresh pasta takes no time to cook, so I suggest you start to prepare the ingredients for the sauce while the water is heating up.

Place the peppercorns in a small dry frying pan over low heat and cook for 3 to 4 minutes, shaking the pan every so often, until the peppercorns become lightly fragrant. Remove and place in a mortar; crush them with a pestle. You want an uneven texture that's coarser than what a pepper mill would give you. If you don't have a mortar and pestle, put the peppercorns on a cutting board, cover them with a napkin or waxed paper and crush them with the back of a heavy frying pan. Put your frying pan back on medium-low heat.

Once your water boils, add some salt, drop in the pasta and give it a stir. The pasta will rise to the surface in 2 to 3 minutes, which means it's ready.

Drain the pasta, reserving 2 cups (500 mL) of the cooking water. Or do what I do: Scoop the pasta right out of the pot with a large spaghetti fork and put it in the frying pan with 1 to 2 cups (250 to 500 mL) of the pasta cooking water. Add the crushed peppercorns and slowly begin to add the cheese, constantly mixing and tossing your pasta thoroughly for a minute or so until it's completely coated, creamy and flecked with the pepper. Serve immediately.

ORECCHIETTE CON RICOTTA E POMODORINI
Orecchiette Pasta with Ricotta and Cherry Tomatoes

This looks like, and is, a simple recipe to make. But the key to its success is getting the freshest and most flavorful ricotta possible. Sheep's milk and cow's milk ricotta both work fine. If you can't find good tomatoes, replace them with a cup or two of Salsa di Cinque Minuti di Mia Mamma (see page 171). I call for cilantro, which is one of my favorite herbs, even though it's not usually part of Italian cuisine, but you can substitute basil, parsley or your favorite herb. Cilantro adds a beautiful fresh pop of flavor and color. This pasta can be served warm or cold. **PER 4 PERSONE**

1 lb (500 g) orecchiette pasta
4 tbsp (60 mL) extra-virgin olive oil, plus extra for drizzling
15 to 20 cherry tomatoes, quartered
Salt, QB
4 oz (125 g) fresh ricotta cheese
1 bunch cilantro, finely chopped

In a pot of boiling water, cook the orecchiette for about 9 minutes or until just before the al dente stage. Drain the pasta, reserving 1 cup (250 mL) of the cooking water.

While the pasta is cooking, heat the olive oil in a frying pan and cook the cherry tomatoes for about a minute, just to soften them a little. Add salt to taste. Add the cooked pasta and ricotta to the pan along with some of the reserved pasta cooking water. This will melt the ricotta and give it a smooth, velvety, creamy consistency.

Sprinkle with cilantro, drizzle with extra-virgin olive oil and serve immediately.

BUCATINI ALL'AMATRICIANA
Bucatini in a Tomato and Pancetta Sauce

This is one of my all-time favorite pastas. Not only does it have the flavor of beautifully crisp pieces of pancetta, but you then use the oil it renders to flavor the rest of the sauce. And as if that wasn't enough, you top it with a good amount of freshly grated pecorino. It's heaven in a bowl.

This is a sauce I refuse to have with any other noodle but bucatini, which is like spaghetti but slightly thicker and hollow. Yes, you can try it with spaghetti if that's all you have, but I urge you to go get some bucatini. It's not hard to find, and you'll get the authentic *all'amatriciana* experience.

You'll note that I've suggested using guanciale, cured Italian pork jowl, even though it's difficult to find in North America. It's the authentic meat used in this Roman classic. But even though I won't bend on the pasta, I will happily use pancetta instead of guanciale. **PER 4 PERSONE**

1 lb (500 g) bucatini pasta
3 tbsp (45 mL) extra-virgin olive oil
6 oz (175 g) guanciale or pancetta, cubed
1 clove garlic, finely chopped
1 small onion, finely chopped
Chili pepper flakes, QB
1 can (19 oz/540 mL) plum tomatoes, crushed
Salt, QB
1 cup (250 mL) grated pecorino cheese

The sauce will cook in about the same time it takes to cook the pasta.

While the pasta is cooking, heat up the olive oil in a frying pan on high heat. Add your guanciale or pancetta and fry until it's crisp, 7 to 10 minutes. Add the garlic, onion and chili pepper flakes and sauté until the onions soften. Turn down the heat to medium-high, add the tomatoes with a little bit of salt and cook for an additional 5 minutes.

Once your pasta is at the al dente stage, reserve a cup of the cooking water, drain the pasta and add it to the sauce. If you're using bucatini, you may not have to add any of the cooking water to the dish because the hollow middle of the noodle traps enough water and will release it right into the sauce. But if you're using spaghetti, I recommend adding some of the liquid to help bind the sauce to the pasta. Let the whole thing cook for about a minute and then remove the pan from the heat. Add the grated pecorino cheese, mix it together and serve.

SOMETHING OUT OF NOTHING

L'Arte di Arrangiarsi

The next few recipes are all about the Italian art of adapting. They are also quintessential *dolce vita* to me because even though they're simple, they're good enough to serve to company. And it goes to show that you don't need a lot of money to open up your kitchen, invite your friends over and bring life into your home.

SPAGHETTI AGLIO E OLIO
Spaghetti with Garlic and Oil

When I was growing up, sometimes my parents would go out for the evening and come home with a group of friends for a midnight snack. One of my parents would go into the kitchen, still dressed in fancy clothes, and whip up spaghetti aglio e olio. Suddenly, my parents seemed glamorous. To me, there's something so *dolce vita* about this memory and this dish.

Aglio e olio is what I call an "un-sauce." But don't take it for granted. There's more of a technique here than you might expect. I've known really good cooks who've messed this up simply by not paying attention. This is a great example of how consciousness and connecting to the food are really important. To make this properly, you're going to do things that are counterintuitive to what you do when making most other pasta dishes. Still, this is probably the fastest sauce ever! Get it right and you're minutes away from creating magic—a little midnight *dolce vita* in your own kitchen.

PER 4 PERSONE

1 lb (500 g) spaghetti
Salt, QB
4 oz (125 g) dry bread crumbs
1 small bunch fresh flat-leaf parsley, finely chopped

1/2 cup (125 mL) extra-virgin olive oil
3 cloves garlic, chopped
Dried chili pepper flakes, QB

Start by cooking your spaghetti. Make sure you salt the water very well. The pasta cooking water is an important ingredient, so when the pasta is done, reserve 2 to 3 cups (500 to 750 mL). While the pasta is cooking, toast the bread crumbs and parsley in a dry saucepan over medium heat until the crumbs are golden. Set them aside.

On medium heat, slowly fry your garlic and chili pepper in the olive oil. You don't want the garlic to cook too fast in oil that's too hot or it will become bitter. What you want is to coax the sweetness out of it. This, of course, will be done way before your spaghetti, so get it off the heat and set it aside.

Once your spaghetti is cooked, you're ready to finish the dish, and this is where you have to pay attention. Traditionally, you'd throw in your pasta and reduce the sauce so that it adheres to the pasta. But if that happens here, you'll dry out your spaghetti and end up adding more olive oil, making the dish way too heavy. So what you're going to do this time is add 1 to 2 cups (250 to 500 mL) of the reserved pasta cooking water to the garlic in the pan, then put in your pasta. Cook this over medium heat for about 1 minute, stirring or tossing it so that the pasta finishes cooking and the starches come out. You've heard that oil and water don't mix. Well, watch this: as the pasta water cooks, it's going to combine with the oil to create a flavorful sauce that coats your spaghetti. Once that happens, you're done.

Divide the pasta among 4 plates. Sprinkle the bread crumb mixture on top. *E basta!*

SPAGHETTI UBRIACHI
Drunken Spaghetti

I first had a version of this recipe at a restaurant in Florence. I loved the way the pasta took on a gorgeous ruby color because of the red wine. When I made it at home, I adapted it by adding some anchovies and finished it by grating a little pecorino over top, which made a perfect salty counterpoint to the sweetness of the red wine. I recommend using a Chianti, but feel free to substitute any good red you have on hand.

1 lb (500 g) spaghetti
4 to 5 cups (1 to 1.25 L) red wine
4 tbsp (60 mL) extra-virgin olive oil
2 cloves garlic, finely chopped
2 anchovies, finely chopped
Chili pepper flakes, QB
1 small bunch fresh flat-leaf parsley, finely chopped
1/4 cup (50 mL) freshly grated pecorino cheese

Boil some water and cook your pasta for about 2 minutes. Drain well.

In a second large pasta pot, put your wine on to boil.

In a frying pan, heat up the olive oil. Add the garlic, anchovies and chili pepper flakes and cook on medium heat until the anchovies melt into the oil and the garlic is brown. Set aside.

Now add your spaghetti to the boiling wine, give it a good stir and finish cooking the pasta until al dente, another 6 or 7 minutes.

When the pasta is ready, the wine will have infused the spaghetti, giving it a gorgeous ruby color. Don't worry about the wine being too strong for the sauce. The alcohol will burn off and leave a sweet delicate taste. Drain spaghetti from the wine, toss in the frying pan with the garlic-anchovy sauce, and finish cooking for 30 seconds. Remove from the heat and sprinkle with a bit of parsley and some grated pecorino.

PER 4 PERSONE

PASTA AL BURRO DI GIOVANNI
Giovanni's Buttered Pasta

This is the dish that all Italian kids are raised on. I ate it, and now I make it for my nephew, Giovanni. It's so simple. In fact, if you want to get your little ones to love cooking, this is a great place to start. Everything is made in one pot, and it's *quanto basta* for all the ingredients. If your kids are still too young to use the stove, you can cook and drain the pasta, give them the other ingredients and let them make it to their own taste. I promise you'll enjoy it, too.   **PER 4 PERSONE**

Penne rigate pasta, unsalted butter, freshly grated Parmigiano-Reggiano cheese, salt (all QB)

Cook and drain the pasta, reserving a little bit of the pasta water. Add the rest of the ingredients, QB, using reserved pasta water as needed and stir. Enjoy.

Un' altra idea: For a grown-up version, use gorgonzola and pecorino cheese. Add them along with the butter so that they melt and form a rich sauce.

SPAGHETTI AL LIMONE
Spaghetti in a Lemon Sauce

The first time I tasted this dish, I was sitting with my buddy Giuseppe on his terrace in Ravello, a gorgeous town on the Amalfi coast. When dinner rolled around, Giuseppe walked out to his backyard and picked a couple of lemons. Within minutes, he'd made one of the best dishes I've ever had. Okay, so it helped that we ate it as the sun set over one of the most beautiful coastlines anywhere on the planet. But I've also eaten it in front of the television, and it was absolutely brilliant.

PER 4 PERSONE

1 lb (500 g) spaghetti
1 clove garlic, for rubbing
2 lemons
5 tbsp (75 mL) extra-virgin olive oil
1 cup (250 mL) freshly grated Parmigiano-Reggiano cheese, plus extra for sprinkling
Salt and freshly ground pepper, QB
1 bunch fresh flat-leaf parsley, chopped
Zest of 1 lemon

Begin by cooking the pasta.

Using raw garlic is tricky. There's nothing worse than biting into a piece of raw garlic. So for this dish, cut the garlic clove in half and rub it in your mixing bowl, then discard it. That way you get just enough of the garlic flavor and not the overpowering bitter taste.

Then it's lemon time: Get the best ones you can. Cut them in half and squeeze the juice into the bowl. With a fork, remove any seeds that have fallen in. Now drizzle your olive oil into the lemon juice, whisking as you go until the mixture emulsifies. Add a good handful of Parmigiano, salt and pepper. Add the parsley and lemon zest.

Drain your pasta and immediately add it to the bowl. Give it a good mix for a minute or so to allow the sauce to combine with the hot spaghetti. You'll see the sauce thicken up and adhere to the spaghetti. Taste it and, if you like, add more Parmigiano.

Un' altra idea: Using the same basic ingredients, make this into a hot version by adding a little olive oil to a saucepan and browning your garlic. Add a can of tuna and freshly squeezed lemon juice. When the spaghetti is ready, add it to the pan and finish off with some Parmigiano. *Buonissimo!*

LASAGNA

Who doesn't love lasagna? But so many people I know avoid making it because they think it's going to take forever and a day. So I've come up with a solution for them. But first, a caveat: There's no way to get around the fact that you have to take time to make a good sauce. Once that's done, this lasagna is easy. You don't even have to boil your sheets of pasta. This is another dish that you can make with your kids. You might want to make extra—it holds really well in the freezer. **PER 6 PERSONE**

6 cups (1.5 L) bolognese sauce (see page 185)
1 lb (500 g) dry lasagna sheets
3 cups (750 mL) béchamel sauce (see page 174)
3 cups (750 mL) or QB shredded mozzarella cheese
Freshly grated Parmigiano-Reggiano cheese, for sprinkling

Spread a bit of the bolognese sauce on the bottom of your lasagna pan. Cover that with a layer of the uncooked lasagna sheets, then a good amount of the bolognese. Drizzle some béchamel sauce on top and sprinkle with some mozzarella. You're going to make 3 or 4 layers, so eyeball the ingredients and layer them accordingly in the same order: pasta, bolognese, béchamel, mozzarella. Use a generous amount of the bolognese sauce, as the liquid is going to cook the raw pasta. Your final layer should be pasta with bolognese sauce. And over top of that, sprinkle your Parmigiano. Be generous. You want the top of the lasagna to get nice and cheesy.

Throw it into a 375°F (190°C) oven and cook for about 40 minutes or until golden on top. Let it rest for about 10 minutes before serving. It tastes better when it's cooled down a bit.

Un' altra idea: There are lots of lasagna variations, and that's exactly how it should be. Everyone should have a signature version. If you want to add bits of ricotta, then add bits of ricotta. You can add slices of boiled egg, pesto—go nuts.

SPAGHETTI ALLA PUTTANESCA DI NONNA MARIA
My Grandma Maria's "Whore's Pasta"

This classic Neapolitan pasta sauce has a suggestive name and a lot of different stories about its origins. The most famous one is that it started as a quick meal for ladies of the night. I've also heard that it was first made on the island of Capri, for the Italian movie star Totò, by a chef who didn't have much left in his kitchen. There are as many stories about how this pasta originated as there are variations. These are two of my favorite things about Italian cooking: the stories about the provenance of the dish, and the fun people have putting their own spin on a classic. This version belongs to my grandmother, who added walnuts to the basic recipe.

The star ingredient of a puttanesca sauce is anchovies. You can also use about a tablespoon (15 mL) of anchovy paste, which I recommend keeping on hand as a staple. Some people are squeamish about the texture of anchovies, whereas a squirt of the paste will dissolve, giving you maximum flavor, and no one will be the wiser.

PER 4 PERSONE

3/4 lb (375 g) spaghetti
4 tbsp (60 mL) extra-virgin olive oil
2 cloves garlic, finely chopped
Dried chili pepper flakes, QB
4 anchovies, roughly chopped,
   or 1 tbsp (15 mL) anchovy paste

2 to 4 tbsp (30 to 60 mL) capers, drained
16 black olives, pitted
1 cup (250 mL) walnuts, roughly chopped
1 can (14oz/398 mL) plum tomatoes, with juices
Salt, QB
Finely chopped fresh flat-leaf parsley, QB

Begin by cooking the pasta. The sauce will be done before the pasta is ready.

Heat the olive oil in a saucepan on medium heat. Throw in the garlic, chili peppers, anchovies or paste, capers, olives and walnuts. Cook gently until the anchovies dissolve and the garlic is lightly browned.

Now, you can use tomato purée, but my preference is plum tomatoes because I like the texture and the look of bits of tomato in the sauce. Put the tomatoes in a bowl and squeeze them with your hands to break them up until you reach a texture you like, then add them to the pan. Cook the sauce, letting it reduce. How much? That's something I'll leave up to you, but you definitely don't want this sauce to be too runny. Now you're going to add some salt, but taste the sauce first. Olives, capers and anchovies are all salty, so what you add now is a matter of taste. Let the sauce simmer for a little while longer. Once the pasta is done, drain it, add it to the saucepan along with a bit of the cooking water, if needed, and let it cook for a minute or so. The sauce will reduce and thicken up. Finish with some chopped parsley.

PASTA E FAGIOLI
Pasta and Beans

Pasta e fagioli—or pasta fazúl—is simply pasta and beans. It's one of my favorites because it's a very hearty and satisfying one-pot meal. Some people think of it as a soup, but I prefer it somewhat drier, as a pasta course, and I eat it with a fork. **PER 4 PERSONE**

2 cups (500 mL) cannellini beans
   (or canned cannellini beans, drained and rinsed)
4 tbsp (60 mL) olive oil
2 cloves garlic, finely chopped
1 small red onion, finely chopped
1 small stalk celery, finely chopped
1 small carrot, finely chopped

3 oz (90 g) pancetta, diced
1 sprig fresh rosemary
3 fresh sage leaves
1/2 lb (250 g) spaghetti
4 1/4 cups (1.05 L) water
1/2 cup (125 mL) freshly grated
   Parmigiano-Reggiano cheese
Extra-virgin olive oil, for drizzling

If you're using dried beans, soak them overnight. Drain. Cover them with fresh water, bring to a boil and simmer for about an hour or until tender.

This starts with a soffritto, so put your pan on medium-high, heat up your olive oil and then add the garlic, onion, celery, carrot, pancetta, rosemary and sage. Cook this until the pancetta and rosemary are nicely browned and crisp.

Next, throw in the beans. Let them cook for a few minutes so they absorb all the flavors. Mash about a quarter of the beans with the back of your spoon. This will help thicken up the dish.

Now comes the pasta. I use spaghetti that I break up into different lengths, but you can use any type you like: penne, tubetti or even a mix. If you have odds and ends, put them in together—it gives the dish some extra personality. Give it all a good stir, then pour in enough of the water to just cover the spaghetti and beans. Let it cook over medium heat for about 20 minutes or until the liquid is reduced and the pasta is cooked. Make sure you stir it every so often so that nothing sticks. I like my pasta e fagioli to be nice and thick. If you want yours to be more like a soup, *va bene,* just add more water.

Let it rest for 10 minutes off the heat. Add the Parmigiano and finish with a drizzle of extra-virgin olive oil. Serve warm.

Un' altra idea: Substitute any legumes, such as lentils or chickpeas, for the beans and you'll have a completely different meal.

SPAGHETTI ALLA CARBONARA
Spaghetti with Bacon and Eggs

This is another iconic Italian dish whose origins are hotly debated. Of all the stories, the one I think is most likely is that the dish was created after World War II. American soldiers, pining for a taste of home, would bring bacon and eggs to their Roman friends. And what do Italians do best? You got it—make pasta! So the clever Italian cooks married the two cultures, and a new classic was born. The one thing that everyone agrees on is that spaghetti alla carbonara was created in Rome. It remains one of that city's signature dishes.

I've been encouraging you to experiment, so trust me when I tell you that the success of this dish relies on using these ingredients only. Forget bacon—use pancetta. Bacon is too heavy, too smoky and too fatty. Plus, the oil that fries the pancetta is going into the dish. The other must is the cheese. You need to use pecorino because the sharp saltiness is what gives this dish a unique flavor.

PER 4 PERSONE

1 lb (500 g) spaghetti
2 tbsp (30 mL) extra-virgin olive oil
2 cloves garlic, finely chopped
3 1/2 oz (100 g) pancetta, cubed

4 eggs
1 cup (250 mL) milk
1/2 cup (125 mL) freshly grated pecorino cheese
Salt and freshly ground pepper, QB

Start cooking the spaghetti. Timing is important here. You want to have everything ready to go when the pasta is finished.

Heat up your olive oil over medium heat. Add the garlic and pancetta and fry until the pancetta is golden and beautifully crisp. When it's done, take the pan off the heat and set it aside.

Now get out 2 bowls and break your eggs, separating the yolks from the whites. To the whites, add the milk, pecorino cheese, salt and lots of pepper, and whisk it all together.

When the spaghetti is ready, drain it well and put it back in the pot but not back on the heat. Throw in your pancetta and flavored oil from the frying pan along with the egg white mixture. Work very fast and stir it all very well for a minute or so to make sure everything is coated. The egg whites will cook in the heat of the pasta and thicken up.

Divide the pasta among 4 serving bowls. On top of each one, plonk a whole uncooked egg yolk and let your guests mix it in. The heat of the pasta mixture will cook the yolks and make it a lot of fun to eat. If you're concerned or squeamish about raw eggs, you can skip the step of separating your eggs and let everything cook in the same pot.

SPAGHETTI ALLA CAPRESE
Capri-Style Spaghetti

Food conjures up memories, and for me this dish is all about summer. Every time I eat it, I'm taken back to some of our holidays along the Amalfi coast. After a hot day at the beach, Nina and I would head back to our friend's hotel in Ravello, the Villa Maria, grab a table on the terrace and order spaghetti alla Caprese. It features an uncooked sauce that takes advantage of the same flavorful ingredients as the Caprese salad and needs only minutes to prepare. This pasta dish can be served hot, or cold like a salad. **PER 4 PERSONE**

1 lb (500 g) spaghetti
2 tomatoes
1/2 lb (250 g) mozzarella di bufala or fior di latte
Salt, QB
4 fresh basil leaves
1 tsp (5 mL) chopped fresh oregano (optional)
1/2 cup (125 mL) extra-virgin olive oil

Begin cooking the pasta.

While it's cooking, cut your tomatoes and mozzarella into cubes and put them in a bowl. Add some salt, then tear up some basil and throw it in. If you want oregano, add it now. I suggest using only fresh; the dried is too overpowering for this dish. Add the olive oil and stir it all together.

When the pasta is done, drain it, reserving a little bit of the cooking water. Put the pasta and the water into your serving bowl, and let it sit for a minute or two to cool down slightly. Then top with the Caprese sauce and serve immediately. Do *not* combine this in the hot pan as I usually suggest for pasta dishes. The mozzarella will melt, and that's not what you're after here. That would make a very different dish—a very good dish, but different.

Risotto

Risotto is a legendary Italian dish. The problem is that the legend comes with a lot of myths. Myth number one: you have to stir until your arm falls off. Number two: if you look away the risotto will burn and form a permanent crust on your pot.

The truth is there's a technique to making risotto that's easy to master. And once you've tried it, you can apply the technique to almost any other risotto.

For a good risotto, I recommend you use a saucepan with a wide base. That way, all the rice is exposed to the bottom of the pan for consistent heating.

One of the big questions about risotto is how much to make. An easy rule of thumb is two handfuls of uncooked rice per person. Now, if you're thinking, "But I have small hands," no problem. Just throw in a little more. If you have any leftovers, they taste good the next day as well.

RISOTTO CON PURÉ DI BARBABIETOLA
Risotto with Beet Purée

This particular recipe will give you a big payoff because it looks so gorgeous, thanks to the beet juice. And if you want to take it one step further, finish with a drizzle of truffle oil to make it extra special.   **PER 4 PERSONE**

1/4 cup (50 mL) extra-virgin olive oil
2 tbsp (30 mL) butter
2 shallots, finely chopped
2 cups (500 mL) Carnaroli or Vialone Nano rice
1 cup (250 mL) white wine
Salt, QB
4 cups (1 L) vegetable stock (see page 151)
2 cups (500 mL) fresh beet juice
Freshly grated Parmigiano-Reggiano cheese, for sprinkling
Truffle oil, for drizzling (optional)

Heat up the olive oil and butter over medium-high heat and sauté the shallots until they're translucent. You don't want to brown them. Add the rice and stir it around to toast it. The rice will become translucent very quickly. At this point, I like to throw in some white wine. Don't worry about putting in too much; the alcohol burns off and the wine adds a light, sweet flavor. The wine is absorbed quickly, and you'll see some of the creamy starch start to be released from the rice. Add some salt. Lower the heat slightly and add a ladleful of the vegetable stock. Give it a light stir and keep your eye on it. Things should be working at a simmer. When the rice has absorbed that first ladleful, add a second, and just keep going, adding the stock as the rice absorbs the liquid. Part of the pleasure of cooking a risotto is tasting it every so often, so you can see it come to life and really find the levels of doneness and flavor that work for you. It takes 16 to 18 minutes to make a risotto.

For this dish, at around the 15-minute mark or just before the al dente stage, add a few ladlefuls of the beet juice. This is going to give the dish a beautiful flavor and a rich color. Once that's absorbed, your dish is pretty much done. There's an expression Italians use when cooking risotto—that you want to create *un' onda,* which means "a wave." That's when the risotto isn't too dry or too watery but has a nice silky kind of wave when you shimmy the pan. So shimmy the pan and taste it. It should be perfectly al dente, with a slight bite to it. You don't want it too runny, too mushy or too dry. You're looking for that balance that is risotto. When you feel you're there, take the pan off the heat. Add your Parmigiano and mix it in.

Now plate the dish and, if you like, finish each serving with a drizzle of truffle oil. Remember, with truffle oil a little goes a long way.

RISOTTO ALLA PUTTANESCA

This is a variation on pasta puttanesca that I came up with one day when I had no pasta on hand and I *really* wanted this sauce. I had a blast making it because I had no idea how it was going to work out. What I've been talking about in this book was what I did. I opened a bottle of wine. I eyeballed the ingredients and connected with the process, tasting as I went—no pressure. It was very *dolce vita*. Not only did it work out really well, but, for a while, it was my new favorite dish. **PER 4 PERSONE**

4 tbsp (60 mL) extra-virgin olive oil,
  plus extra for drizzling
1 shallot, finely diced
4 anchovies, roughly chopped,
  or 1 tbsp (15 mL) anchovy paste
2 to 4 tbsp (30 to 60 mL) capers, drained
12 black olives, pitted and halved
Chili pepper flakes, QB

2 cups (500 mL) Carnaroli or Vialone Nano rice
1 cup (250 mL) white wine
2 cups (500 mL) tomato purée
4 to 5 cups (1 to 1.25 L) water or vegetable
  stock, heated to a simmer
Salt, QB
Finely chopped fresh flat-leaf parsley, QB
1/2 cup (125 mL) pine nuts, toasted

In a risotto pan or a saucepan with a large bottom, heat the olive oil over medium-high heat. Add the shallots, anchovies or anchovy paste, capers, olives and chili pepper flakes and cook gently until the shallots are slightly browned. At this point, add your rice, giving it a good stir. You want the rice to toast a bit and to absorb all the flavors.

Throw in the wine and stir. It will be absorbed quickly. Now add the tomato purée. Again, stir it a bit and keep your eye on it. In a few minutes, the whole thing will get thick as the rice starts to absorb and take on that intense tomato flavor.

Now you have to start adding your liquid. Most risottos call for a flavorful stock. But when I came up with this dish, I didn't have any on hand and decided to use water. The ingredients were so flavorful that I figured they would be enough, and I was right! So at this stage, if you're not using vegetable stock, that's okay; you can feel confident using water. Lower the heat to medium and pour in the water a cup at a time, adding more when it's absorbed. Add salt as needed. You'll be doing this for the next 16 to 18 minutes, until the risotto is al dente, not too liquid nor too dry, and creates a bit of *un' onda*, or a wave, when you lightly shimmy the pan. You can also taste it to see if it's as you like it.

Remove it from the heat and add the parsley, a drizzle of olive oil and half of the pine nuts. Use the rest of the pine nuts to garnish each serving.

"RISOTTO" DI FARRO
Spelt Cooked "Risotto Style"

Farro is an ancient grain that's similar to the wheat berry, barley and spelt. It has made a major comeback in Italy in recent years. Farro has a chewy texture and nutty taste, and it has the added benefit of being naturally organic. If it's sprayed with pesticides, it won't grow. If you can find it, you can use farro where you'd use rice or pasta in soups, salads or a risotto-style dish.
PER 4 PERSONE

1/4 cup (50 mL) extra-virgin olive oil
2 tbsp (30 mL) unsalted butter, divided
3 shallots, finely chopped
3/4 lb (375 g) spelt or wheat berries

3 cups (750 mL) Chianti Classico wine
2 cups (500 mL) vegetable stock, heated to a simmer
Salt and freshly ground pepper, QB
Freshly grated Parmigiano-Reggiano cheese, QB

If you've made traditional risotto, you can make this recipe—no problem. It will take 3 or 4 minutes longer, but really, that's just another sip of wine and a few more stirs. As with any basic risotto, you're going to start by pouring olive oil into your pan. But, in this case, you're going to use 1 tbsp (15 mL) butter as well to help give some extra creaminess to the finished dish. When the butter is melted, add your shallots and sauté until they're translucent. Then add the spelt, a couple of handfuls per serving, and mix it up so that it toasts and absorbs the butter and oil mixture.

Next comes the wine. I recommend that you use a Chianti Classico, but any full-bodied red wine will work in this dish. Add a bit to start, and pour yourself a glass. Get comfortable—you're sticking around for 20 to 25 minutes. Stir gently while the wine evaporates. Then ladle in your vegetable stock—not too much, just a bit to get things going. And give it a stir. Once the stock is absorbed, add a little more and some salt and pepper. And 1 or 2 more ladlefuls of stock, one at a time.

Now you're at the halfway point, and it's going to get really fun. Time to switch from stock to vino. Add a good splash to the pot and stir that around. You're going to keep going like this—when the splash is absorbed, add another. After a few good splashes, the spelt will start to puff up, and that's the signal for you to start tasting. Just keep adding the wine until your taste tells you that the grain is done. Don't worry if it seems that you're adding a lot of wine. There have been occasions when I've made this dish with just wine and no stock, and it's been fine. Well, actually, very good. It's a bit of an indulgence. But back to the point: the alcohol burns off, leaving a beautifully delicate, sweet taste. Once you're happy with its doneness, take the pot off the heat.

Because spelt is a grain that doesn't give off a lot of starch the way rice does, we're going to help it along by adding the remaining 1 tbsp (15 mL) butter and a good handful of Parmigiano to finish—to give it more of that risotto-like texture and, of course, flavor.

RISOTTO SPINACI DI ORSOLA
Orsola's Spinach Risotto

I learned this dish from a friend in Rome. She's the sister of a dear friend and, in the Italian fashion, insisted we call her when we got to town, which we did. She immediately invited us over for dinner and wouldn't take no for an answer. We arrived just as she was getting home from work. She greeted us as if she'd known us forever and made us this dish she whipped up in her tiny kitchen in no time. It was incredible, homey and comforting, almost a cross between a soup and a risotto. She calls this her lazy risotto, because when time is short or when she's tired, she turns to this dish. Now it's a staple in my kitchen when I want risotto but can't give it the attention it requires. It's not a true risotto—it's a little heavier, but delicious. It's simple enough to make one serving for yourself when you're feeling tired, yet good enough for when you need to make *una bella figura.*

So here's how you make it. Get a big pot and throw in some Arborio rice. You're going to cook the rice almost as you would any long-grain rice, so add 4 times the volume of water to rice, and some salt. Bring it to a boil, lower the heat to medium and let it simmer, stirring it every so often. While the rice is cooking, chop up some spinach. You can use either fresh or frozen, defrosted of course, and sauté it in a pan with some olive oil, garlic and salt. When the spinach is soft and wilted, transfer it to a food processor, adding a little bit of water, and purée it.

At this point, the rice should be almost done, and you should still have some water in the pot. Drain off all but a third of the excess water. Add the spinach purée, 3 generous tbsp (45 mL) of ricotta cheese, a good handful of Parmigiano and 1 tbsp (15 mL) butter if you like, for added creaminess. Lower the heat and mix until everything blends with the rice and it looks creamy and silky like a good risotto. Cook a little bit longer to let the flavors combine. Depending on the style of dish you want, you can actually cook it longer to let it dry out like a regular risotto, or you can leave it a bit soupier if that seems like a good idea to you. I like mine slightly runnier than a risotto.

The reason this dish works so well is that the starchy water from cooking the rice gives it all a creamy risotto texture. As you've noticed, in this recipe I haven't given you any quantities. I want to encourage you to just go into the kitchen and eyeball, throwing in as much as you'd like. I promise you will have maximum results! To make your life simple, here's a list of the ingredients. All of them are *quanto basta,* of course.

Arborio rice, water, fresh spinach, extra-virgin olive oil, garlic, salt, ricotta and freshly grated Parmigiano-Reggiano cheese, butter

POLENTA

Polenta is cornmeal that's been cooked in water. In certain parts of Italy, especially in the north, it's used more than pasta. In Veneto and Friuli, for example, it's served as a side dish or anti-pasto. It can be prepared in a million ways, from something resembling mashed potatoes to a dense corn bread. It can be fried, baked or grilled. As you've probably figured out, all of these versions are comfort foods.

There are two types of polenta—white and yellow cornmeal—and each has its own texture. There's the coarse one, which is like sand, and the very fine one, which is like flour. I prefer the coarse one because I like the grainier texture and find that it has more flavor.   **PER 8 PERSONE**

8 cups (2 L) lukewarm salted water
1 lb (500 g) coarse-grain polenta
Salt, QB
Freshly grated Parmigiano-Reggiano cheese, QB
Extra-virgin olive oil, for drizzling

You want to start with lukewarm water. Cold water will make the polenta very lumpy, which, needless to say, is not a good thing. Put the water in a pot over high heat. With one hand, pour in the polenta in an even stream while whisking constantly with the other. When all the polenta is mixed in, add some salt. Stir a little more. Once it starts to boil, lower the heat to medium. Stir every few minutes until the polenta bubbles up and goes *blop, blop, blop.* Lower the heat again and let it cook for another 20 to 25 minutes, stirring every few minutes so it doesn't stick. Taste will tell you when it's done. It should have the texture of a cooked purée: fluffy yet dense. It's hard to describe, but as with porridge, you'll know the difference between cooked and uncooked.

Once it's done, take it off the heat. You can serve it immediately as is, with a little bit of freshly grated Parmigiano and olive oil. Or ladle it onto individual plates and spoon some tomato sauce on top.

If you want a firmer version, pour the polenta onto a clean work board and spread it out so that it's about 1 inch (2.5 cm) thick. It will cool quickly. Let it set for half an hour, then slice it. You can serve the slices as is, or grill, bake or fry them.

oVinaio
SAVEUR
La Cucaracha
COCKTAIL CLUB
famous the WORLD
ARRIORS

Street Life

Go to any town in Italy on a Sunday from about four to six in the afternoon and the streets are absolutely packed. Mothers and fathers pushing strollers, and *nonni* with the grandchildren. Even teenagers, maybe walking a few feet behind their parents, but they're out there after the Sunday *pranzo per fare una passeggiata.* It's one of the simple pleasures, a key to the *dolce vita* of everyday life: getting outside, connecting to your community, taking in the life of the city.

People get dressed up so that they feel good, to show their pride—who doesn't feel better when dressed well?—and also to make *una bella figura* as they connect with neighbors, friends and family. It's a simple thing, but it has a kind of allure to it. People head down to the piazza and watch the parade. Generally, the walk will take them to the bar or the *pasticceria,* where they'll have an espresso and a slice of torta, or maybe a little gelato.

La Vineria e l'Aperitivo

Italian customs seem to have been created to allow for *dolce vita* moments every d
lunch, for instance, you'll find people stopping by the bar for a little glass of wine
small portion, and a panino, priced so that anyone can enjoy it. This isn't about gett
maximum amount of alcohol in you in a single day. It's about small luxuries, a sensua
rience in the middle of the day. For me, the art of *dolce vita* doesn't need to be extrav
It's taking a few moments to slow down, to indulge your senses and reconnect with y
and those around you.

For me, the art of *dolce vita* includes balance.

Secondi

This section needs little introduction. It contains a collection of heartier dishes that are traditionally thought of as main courses. These are your *secondi,* your entrées. At an Italian meal, you serve *i secondi* with a selection of sides of your choice, to complement flavor and texture.

SPIEDINI ALLA GRIGLIA
Rolled Stuffed Veal Skewers on the Grill

Have you ever been to the butcher's or your fishmonger's and been overwhelmed by what you've seen and not known what to make for dinner? Start a conversation with these guys. Most of them are foodies, and they have tons of recipes. Not only will they be happy to pass one along to you, but the next time you go in, they'll holler and ask you how it turned out. After making friends with these guys, I can't tell you how many times they either redirected me to a better cut or a better bargain or went into the back to get something they'd set aside for their special customers. It makes the whole shopping experience so much more fun.

This recipe came out of a conversation I had with a butcher in Palermo. We started talking about food, and he shared what he was making for dinner that night. Inspired by his recipe, I adapted it to suit my own tastes. Any stuffed dish is a perfect example of what I've been saying about *quanto basta* and making dishes your own. Each of these ingredients is so flavorful that there should be no pressure about getting it right. It's just about assembly and a couple of other ingredients to bind them together.

PER 4 PERSONE

3 oz (90 g) cooked ham, minced
3 oz (90 g) Emmenthal cheese, finely chopped
3 oz (90 g) Parmigiano-Reggiano cheese, finely grated
3 oz (90 g) caciocavallo cheese or any sheep's milk cheese, finely chopped
1/2 cup (125 mL) dry bread crumbs
1/2 cup (125 mL) pine nuts
1/2 cup (125 mL) raisins
1 bunch fresh flat-leaf parsley, chopped
1/4 cup (50 mL) extra-virgin olive oil
2 lb (1 kg) thinly sliced veal medallions, pounded thin
1 red onion, quartered and pulled apart into layers
24 fresh bay leaves
Wooden skewers, soaked in cool water for at least an hour

For the stuffing: In a large mixing bowl, combine the prosciutto cotto, or cooked ham, all three cheeses, bread crumbs, pine nuts, raisins and parsley. Add a good splash of olive oil, which, along with the bread crumbs, binds everything together. Now get your hands in there and mix it up. Taste it to make sure you're happy.

Now the fun starts. Lay out a slice of the veal. Get a small palmful of stuffing and roll it in your hands until it's a compact oval. Put the stuffing on the slice of veal and roll it up, starting by folding in the sides, then rolling from the top to the bottom. You want to make sure the stuffing is sealed in and won't fall apart when you put it on the grill. Continue until you've used up all of your ingredients. You should have 12 veal rolls.

Take a wooden skewer and start assembling the spiedini: First skewer a layer of onion, then a bay leaf. On goes your veal roll. Pierce the meat at the final fold so that it doesn't unravel. Then finish off the skewer with another layer of onion and another bay leaf. Sandwiching the veal in this way will add even more flavor, not that it needs much more. Place the spiedini on your barbecue and cook them for about 5 minutes on each side.

Un' altra idea: If you don't have a barbecue, simply sear your spiedini in a hot frying pan with some oil for about a minute or so on each side. Splash in some white wine to help deglaze the pan, then transfer the pan to a hot oven. Finish cooking for 5 minutes.

FILETTO DI MANZO CON SOFFRITTO
Beef Tenderloin with Soffritto

Forget about heavy sauces. If you have a really good piece of meat, just keep it simple. Here, a flavorful soffritto (see page 153) is used as a topping to add a little extra something. It's always been a favorite at my dinner parties. And it can even be served at room temperature.   **PER 4 PERSONE**

For the soffritto:
1/4 cup (50 mL) olive oil
1 onion, chopped
2 medium carrots, chopped
2 stalks celery, chopped
4 cloves garlic
2 sprigs fresh rosemary
4 fresh sage leaves
2 fresh bay leaves
Salt and freshly ground pepper, QB

4 lb (2 kg) beef tenderloin
Salt and freshly ground pepper, QB
Extra-virgin olive oil, QB
1 cup (250 mL) white wine

Begin by making your classic soffritto. Because it's going to be the sauce, I generally cut my vegetables larger than I would for my soups or stews. I like to add garlic as well as fresh herbs, such as rosemary sprigs, sage leaves and bay leaves.

Grab a big sauté pan and, over medium-high heat, pour in the olive oil. When that's heated up, add the onions, carrots, celery, garlic, fresh herbs, and salt and pepper. Cook until the vegetables become soft and golden.

While the vegetables are cooking, season your meat with salt and pepper. When the soffritto is done, remove the vegetables from the pan, leaving as much oil as possible. Return the pan to high heat and, if necessary, add a splash of olive oil. Now sear the tenderloin on all sides. Add the wine and the soffritto and cook until the wine reduces, which will take a minute or so. Transfer the beef to a cutting board and slice it into fairly thick pieces. Put it on a serving dish and spoon the soffritto over top.

This preparation is for medium-rare. If you want the meat well done, slice the tenderloin while it's medium-rare. Remove the pan from the heat and put the sliced tenderloin back into the pan for a few minutes, where it will continue to cook in the juices.

FILETTO DI MANZO AL BALSAMICO
Beef Tenderloin with Balsamic Reduction

Beef tenderloin, salt and freshly ground pepper, extra-virgin olive oil, balsamic vinegar, onions

When you're using a good beef tenderloin, you don't want to cover it with heavy sauces. Season with a little salt and pepper. Heat up a pan with some olive oil and place the tenderloin in it. Cook it to the degree of doneness that suits your taste. I think this cut of beef should be eaten medium-rare, so I recommend cooking it for a minute or two on each side.

When the meat is done to your liking, you can either remove it or leave it in for this next step. Turn the heat to high and add a good splash (4 to 5 tbsp/60 to 75 mL) of balsamic vinegar for each piece of tenderloin. This deglazes the pan and, as it reduces, creates a beautiful thick, sweet sauce. The good news is that you can use a less expensive balsamic for this sauce.

If you want to add caramelized onions: Before you cook the meat, cut your onions into thin slices and throw them into a hot pan with some olive oil on medium heat. Add some salt and pepper and let the onions cook until they become soft, sweet and golden, which should take about 10 minutes. When you serve the dish, arrange the onions on top of the meat and drizzle with the balsamic sauce.

BRACIOLE DI NONNA MARIA
My Grandmother Maria's Rolled Beef

It's funny how food brings back such strong memories. Walking along streets in Florence, I would catch the smell of tomato sauce when a trattoria door opened, and it would take me right back to my childhood. I grew up on the sweet smell of a meat and tomato sauce simmering on the stove. This dish also makes me think about the simple brilliance of Italian cooking. In this case, you have the sauce for one course and the main cooking together, lending their flavors to each other and giving off the most intoxicating aroma.

Braciole are rolled stuffed meat, cooked slowly for several hours in tomato sauce. On the surface, it looks like a gourmet meal, but it comes from the past, when most families couldn't afford much meat. So that's where you find the inventiveness of the Italian mother who wanted to feed her family well. She'd figure out how to make a little bit of meat go a long way. By cooking it in tomato sauce, the result would be a meat-flavored pasta sauce for the primo, as well as a beautifully moist and tender piece of meat for the secondo. It was the power of imagination and alchemy. What brilliance!

PER 4 PERSONE

2 lb (1 kg) flank steak, cut into 1/2-inch (1 cm) slices
1 bunch fresh flat-leaf parsley, chopped
1/2 cup (125 mL) raisins
1/2 cup (125 mL) pine nuts
Salt and freshly ground pepper, QB

1/4 cup (50 mL) extra-vigin olive oil
2 cloves garlic, finely chopped
1 cup (250 mL) red wine
4 cups (1 L) tomato purée
Fresh basil leaves, QB (optional)

Ask your butcher for some sliced beef. Either he can flatten it for you or you can do it at home. If you're doing it at home, put each slice between 2 pieces of plastic wrap and go to it with a meat pounder.

Put the meat on a cutting board and place the chopped parsley, raisins and pine nuts in the middle of each slice. Sprinkle with salt and pepper. Roll up the meat like a jelly roll, with all the ingredients inside, and use toothpicks to hold the rolls together.

On high heat, coat the bottom of a large saucepan with olive oil and add the garlic and braciole. Sear the meat on all sides until it turns golden brown. Add some red wine to the pan to deglaze the bits of meat stuck to the bottom. Let reduce. Add the tomato purée and salt to the pan and simmer for 2 hours. If you like, tear up some basil and sprinkle it on after the dish is fully cooked.

At this point, you've created a perfect meat-flavored tomato sauce. You can serve your braciole with a little bit of the sauce or on its own.

SPEZZATINO DI MANZO
Classic Beef Stew

This is another one-pot recipe with brilliant results. In my opinion, the most important part of many one-pot wonders is the flavor base, which is the soffritto.

This is a great dish to make when you're hanging around the house, because it gets its flavor from a long, slow cooking time. And the good news is that you can ask your butcher for a cheaper or inferior cut of meat to make it. That's probably why some people call this the poor man's stew.

PER 4 PERSONE

2 lb (1 kg) stewing beef, cut into 1-inch (2.5 cm) cubes
1/2 cup (125 mL) extra-virgin olive oil
Salt and freshly ground pepper, QB
1 large carrot, finely chopped
1 large stalk celery, finely chopped
1 onion, finely chopped
3 cups (750 mL) red wine
1/2 cup (125 mL) tomato purée
2 large potatoes, peeled and cut into large pieces
Vegetable stock or water, QB (optional)

The first thing you want to do is sear the stewing beef to give it a nice crust. So heat up your pan on high heat, add the olive oil and then add the meat, cooking it for a few minutes in the hot oil until the outside gets nice and brown. Transfer it to a plate, season it with some salt and pepper, and set it aside.

Lower the heat to medium-high and add a splash of olive oil, then the soffritto ingredients: the carrot, celery and onions. Stir this around, mixing everything together. You'll notice that some bits of meat are stuck to the bottom of the pan, so throw in a cup of the red wine to deglaze the pan and stir, scraping up those bits of fat and meat, which are full of flavor. Let that reduce and cook until it gets soft and golden.

Throw your meat back in and mix everything together. Add the rest of the wine, the tomato purée, and salt and pepper. Let the liquid come to a slight boil and throw in the potatoes. I like to cut my potatoes into big chunks so that they don't break down over the long cooking time and become a big *pappa.* Make sure everything is covered by the liquid. If your vegetables and meat aren't fully covered, you can add vegetable stock. Or if you don't have any stock, water is fine. Turn the heat down to medium and let it cook for about 1 1/2 hours, stirring every so often so that it doesn't stick. The liquid will cook down and give the spezzatino a rich, thick sauce.

POLPETTE SAPORITE
Tasty Meatballs

This is the first of three recipes featuring another icon of Italian cooking: the meatball. Everyone loves meatballs. They're easy to make. In Italy, meatballs vary from region to region, even from house to house. For instance, my two grandmothers made totally different ones. And growing up, I realized that it was a bit of a reflection of their own personalities! One was a little softer and the other a bit harder; one's meatballs were light and moist, the other's heavier and more rustic. But I could never have picked my favorite. I loved them equally. This recipe pays tribute to both my *nonne* but with my own touch—the addition of raisins and pine nuts. Once you get the hang of the basics, feel free to put your spin on them to make your own *polpette classiche*.

There are a few ways to make meatballs. You can fry them, then cook them in tomato sauce. Or you can simmer them from a raw state right in a simple tomato sauce; that way, the meat also flavors the sauce. Whichever way you choose to cook them, essentially the meatballs will be as good as the ingredients you use. So the more flavor you put into them, the more flavorful they'll be.

The best thing about making meatballs is that they're really *quanto basta*. It's about eyeballing everything you put into the mixing bowl. The star is your meat; the rest is your supporting cast. Funny thing is that when I go to the butcher shop, I don't ask for a pound of this or that. I ask him to put the meat on the scale a handful at a time until I see whether it's enough or not! Perhaps that's because I look at cooking as a fun visual thing rather than a technical thing. Maybe this is on my mind because we're going to put everything in a bowl where you can eyeball it and see how much of any ingredient looks right. If I'd had had my way, I would have given you just a list of my suggested ingredients and let you go nuts. But my editor would have killed me! For those of you who prefer a first-time guide, I've given you some proportions I like. But feel free to let your eyes and your taste buds guide you. What's the worst thing that can happen? The next time you make meatballs, you make adjustments. Great! This really is about the pleasure of cooking.

2 or 3 slices Italian bread, crusts removed
1 cup (250 mL) milk
1 lb (500 g) ground beef
1 lb (500 g) ground pork
1/2 cup (125 mL) raisins (optional)
1/2 cup (125 mL) pine nuts (optional)
2 eggs
1 cup (250 mL) freshly grated Parmigiano-Reggiano cheese
1 bunch fresh flat-leaf parsley, finely chopped (optional)
4 fresh basil leaves, finely chopped
Salt and freshly ground pepper, QB
Extra-virgin olive oil, for browning

For the sauce:
1/2 cup (125 mL) extra-virgin olive oil
1 small onion, chopped
1 cup (250 mL) red wine
4 cups (1 L) tomato purée
Salt and freshly ground pepper, QB

PER 6–8 PERSONE

So first thing, soak your crustless bread in milk. You want it to really soak up the liquid. Get a big bowl so you can really get your hands in there when it's time to mix. Put in the ground beef and pork, raisins and pine nuts. Of course, if you don't like raisins or pine nuts, or don't have them, it's okay to leave them out. The dish will still be tasty without them. I find raisins give a real sweetness to the dish, but make sure you use nice, fresh plump ones here. Don't think that just because they're going to get cooked you can use the old ones that are stuck to the bottom of the jar!

Now add the eggs and Parmigiano, which will help bind everything together. Some meatball recipes use bread crumbs, but they can sometimes make the meatballs too dense. So to make ours nice and moist, we're using the bread soaked in milk. But before you add it, squeeze the bread to remove most of the milk.

Break the squeezed bread into little pieces and add them to the bowl. Add the chopped parsley, if you're using it, basil, salt and pepper. Roll up your sleeves, get your hands in there and start mixing—I mean *really* mixing. You want everything combined as evenly as possible and then some. Once all the ingredients are mixed well, start rolling them up into little balls about the size of golf balls. You don't want to make them too big or they'll take a long time to cook.

If you're frying them: Slightly flatten the little balls, lightly pressing with your hand so that they're not quite like patties but will fry more evenly. Then heat the olive oil in your frying pan. When the oil is hot, add the meatballs and cook until they're browned on each side. They can be served immediately or with a little bit of tomato sauce poured right over them, or they can be put in your simmering tomato sauce for a few minutes.

To cook them in sauce: You can use either the Salsa di Cinque Minuti di Mia Mamma (see page 171) or this version, which is just as simple. Heat up some olive oil in a pan, add the onions and cook until they're soft and slightly brown. Add some red wine and let it cook for a minute so that the alcohol can burn off, then add the tomato purée and salt and pepper. When the mixture comes to a boil, lower the heat to maintain a gentle simmer and carefully add the uncooked meatballs. Allow this to simmer away for about an hour. I promise you'll have one of the best sauces ever.

If you use the tomato sauce method to cook your meatballs, I suggest breaking up a couple of them so that when you serve the sauce with your pasta it has little bits of meat, just as a tease. Reserve the rest of your meatballs for the secondo part of the meal. Perfect for the Sunday *pranzo*.

POLPETTE CON FOGLIE DI LIMONE
Meatballs Cooked with Lemon Leaves

I was first served these meatballs in Sicily, where lemons are a big part of the cuisine. Even in a country where variations are a part of the tradition, this method is a bit unusual. The meat was sandwiched between two lemon leaves and cooked on a barbecue. The lemon leaves kept the moisture in, while the oils infused the meat with a hint of lemon. Now, I know that lemon leaves may not be the easiest thing to find. But the good news is that you can substitute lemon zest. Or if you can get orange or grapefruit leaves, they will work nicely, too.

Although there are some barbecue recipes that work equally well in an oven or in a grill pan, I don't recommend trying that with this one.   **PER 4 PERSONE**

2 lb (1 kg) lean ground beef
1 bunch fresh flat-leaf parsley, chopped
1 cup (250 mL) freshly grated Parmigiano-Reggiano cheese
1 cup (250 mL) fine dry bread crumbs
1 tsp (5 mL) freshly grated nutmeg
Sea salt and freshly ground pepper, QB
3/4 cup (175 mL) milk
Zest of 1 lemon
1/4 cup (50 mL) extra-virgin olive oil
Large lemon leaves, 2 per meatball (optional)

You'll be mixing this with your hands, so grab a big mixing bowl. Put in the beautifully lean ground beef, chopped parsley, Parmigiano, bread crumbs, nutmeg, salt and pepper. Add the milk, which helps moisten and soften the meatballs, the lemon zest, and the olive oil, which will give it nice flavor. Now mix the whole thing up with your hands. You want to make sure that all the ingredients are well combined.

Make your meatballs slightly larger than golf balls, then flatten them like patties. This will help the meat cook more evenly when it's on the grill. If you're using the lemon leaves, sandwich each patty between 2 lemon leaves. Place on the barbecue and grill on high heat for about 5 minutes per side. Don't worry—the lemon leaves won't burn. When they're done, discard the leaves and enjoy the most flavorful, moist, flattened meatballs ever.

POLPETTE DI ACCIUGHE
Anchovy Meatballs

Okay, I'm going to deal with this upfront because this is a dish I think you should try. Outside of the Mediterranean, anchovies are controversial. They aren't the fish of choice for most people. But fresh anchovies really are wonderful. They have a sweet and delicate taste, not at all fishy.

I made this "meatball" for a group of friends, including one who claimed to hate fish. She tasted it and fell in love and wanted the recipe. She was shocked when she found out that this flavorful little meatball was made of anchovies.

Fresh anchovies can be difficult to find. But if you know your fishmonger and you're able to ask him to order some in, do so. It's definitely worth the effort. If you can't find fresh anchovies, the good news is that you can substitute fresh tuna or fresh swordfish. PER 4 PERSONE

2 lb (1 kg) fresh anchovies, cleaned and chopped
3/4 cup (175 mL) dry bread crumbs
1 egg
2 cloves garlic, finely chopped
1 bunch fresh flat-leaf parsley, finely chopped
3/4 cup (175 mL) freshly grated Parmigiano-Reggiano cheese
Salt, QB
1 cup (250 mL) white wine
Extra-virgin olive oil, for frying
Tomato sauce, QB (optional)

Here's the thing I didn't mention above. Now that I've convinced you to try this dish, I have to be honest. You may not be able to find fresh anchovies that are cleaned, which means you'll have to do it yourself. And by clean I mean that you take your anchovy in your hands, twist the head and yank. In that one move, the guts and innards should come out. Discard. Then cut open the anchovy, remove the tail and scrape away the skin with a knife.

When you're done, rinse the anchovies under cold water and you're ready to go. (Okay, maybe at this point you'll decide you want to use tuna or swordfish!) Now chop the anchovies into little pieces so they look like the minced meat you'd use for regular meatballs. Put them in a big bowl and add the bread crumbs, egg, garlic, parsley, Parmigiano and salt. Finish by adding some white wine. With this recipe, it's all about texture. Get your hands in the bowl and mix it all together to a nice even consistency. You don't want the mixture to be too wet or dry. If it gets too dry, just add a little more wine.

Start rolling the mixture into little balls, about the size of golf balls. It's a good idea to have a bowl of water in front of you so that if the mixture gets a little sticky you can wet your hands a bit. Make sure the balls are nice and compact so they won't fall apart when you're frying them.

Heat up some olive oil in a saucepan. In batches, fry the balls for a couple of minutes on each side until they're golden on the outside and cooked through. As you take them out, put them on a paper towel to absorb some of the excess oil. You can serve them as is or add them to a simple tomato sauce to cook for a few minutes so the flavors marry. Serve them as a main course after your pasta.

SALSICCIE E FAGIOLI
Pork 'n' Beans

To me, this dish evokes the time of year when the days get shorter and a chill sets in. You naturally want to eat more comforting foods but don't necessarily have the time or energy to fuss. This classic Tuscan dish is a one-pot wonder. For the most part, you can make it with essentials from your pantry. Stop by your butcher to get some sausages, pick up some fresh rosemary and *basta!* You're about half an hour away from an amazing meal. **PER 4 PERSONE**

4 tbsp (60 mL) extra-virgin olive oil
3 cloves garlic, finely chopped
8 pork sausages, each about 3 oz (90 g)
2 sprigs fresh rosemary
Splash red wine
1 can (10 oz/284 mL) plum tomatoes, with juices
2 cans (each 19 oz/540 mL) cannelli or white navy beans, drained and rinsed
Salt and freshly ground pepper, QB

Start off by heating the olive oil in your pot. You're going to use less oil than you might usually use because the sausages will give off a lot of fat as they cook. Then into the heated oil put your garlic, sausages and rosemary sprig. I like to throw the whole sprig in at this stage. The rosemary gets crisp and eventually those pieces break off and infuse the dish with flavor. Just remove the stem before serving.

Cook the sausages for a few minutes and pierce them with the end of a knife to let some of the fat out. That will flavor the dish as well. Once the sausages are browned, pour a glass of red wine, take a sip and throw the rest in. Then add the plum tomatoes with all their juices and let the whole thing simmer for a bit. As it's simmering, use a fork or the back of a spoon to break up the tomatoes. You could use tomato purée, but I prefer this dish chunkier. Let it simmer for about 10 minutes or until slightly reduced.

Add the beans to the pan. Add salt and pepper and let the whole thing reduce and thicken, about another 15 minutes, stirring occasionally to make sure nothing sticks. You can thicken it more by mashing up a third of the beans.

Un' altra idea: Substitute lentils for the cannelli beans.

SALSICCIA CON CIME DI RAPA
Pork Sausage with Rapini

Cime di rapa, le rape, i rapini and *broccoli di rape* are the various names Italians have for rapini. This bitter, leafy green is one of my favorite vegetables. Blanched in boiling water and sautéed in olive oil and garlic, it's incredible. This is one of those all-in-one meals in which you get your main and your side together.   **PER 4 PERSONE**

1 large bunch rapini
5 tbsp (75 mL) extra-virgin olive oil
3 cloves garlic, finely chopped
Whole chili peppers, QB
Salt, QB
8 pork sausages, each about 3 oz (90 g)

Wash the rapini in cold water, cut it into small pieces and throw it in a big pot of boiling salted water. It may look like a lot of rapini but, like spinach, it cooks down considerably, so always get more than you think you need. And honestly, who cares if there's extra? This stuff tastes amazing the next day in a sandwich with some great cheese. Cook the rapini for a couple of minutes, drain it well and set it aside.

Heat a saucepan over high heat, add a good amount of olive oil and brown the garlic and chili peppers. Then add your rapini, tossing it a few times over high heat. Lower the heat to medium, add some salt, and let it cook for a few minutes, tossing it every so often.

Set another frying pan on medium-high heat. Add a little bit of olive oil. Put your sausages in and let them get brown on the outside, then pierce them each a couple of times to release some of the fat. Lower the heat to medium and continue until they're cooked through. If you find that your sausages are sticking to the pan, don't add more oil, just a splash of water.

When the sausages are cooked through, add them to the other pan to meet their new mates, and cook together for a few minutes.

Un' altra idea: Cook up some orecchiette pasta. While that's cooking, cut the rapini and sausages into small pieces. When the pasta is done, drain the water, reserving about a cup, put the orecchiette back into the pot with the reserved pasta water, rapini and sausage, and cook it for another minute or so, letting the water reduce. Then add a drizzle of olive oil and a sprinkle of Parmigiano-Reggiano cheese. Now you have orecchiette con cime di rapa e salsicce.

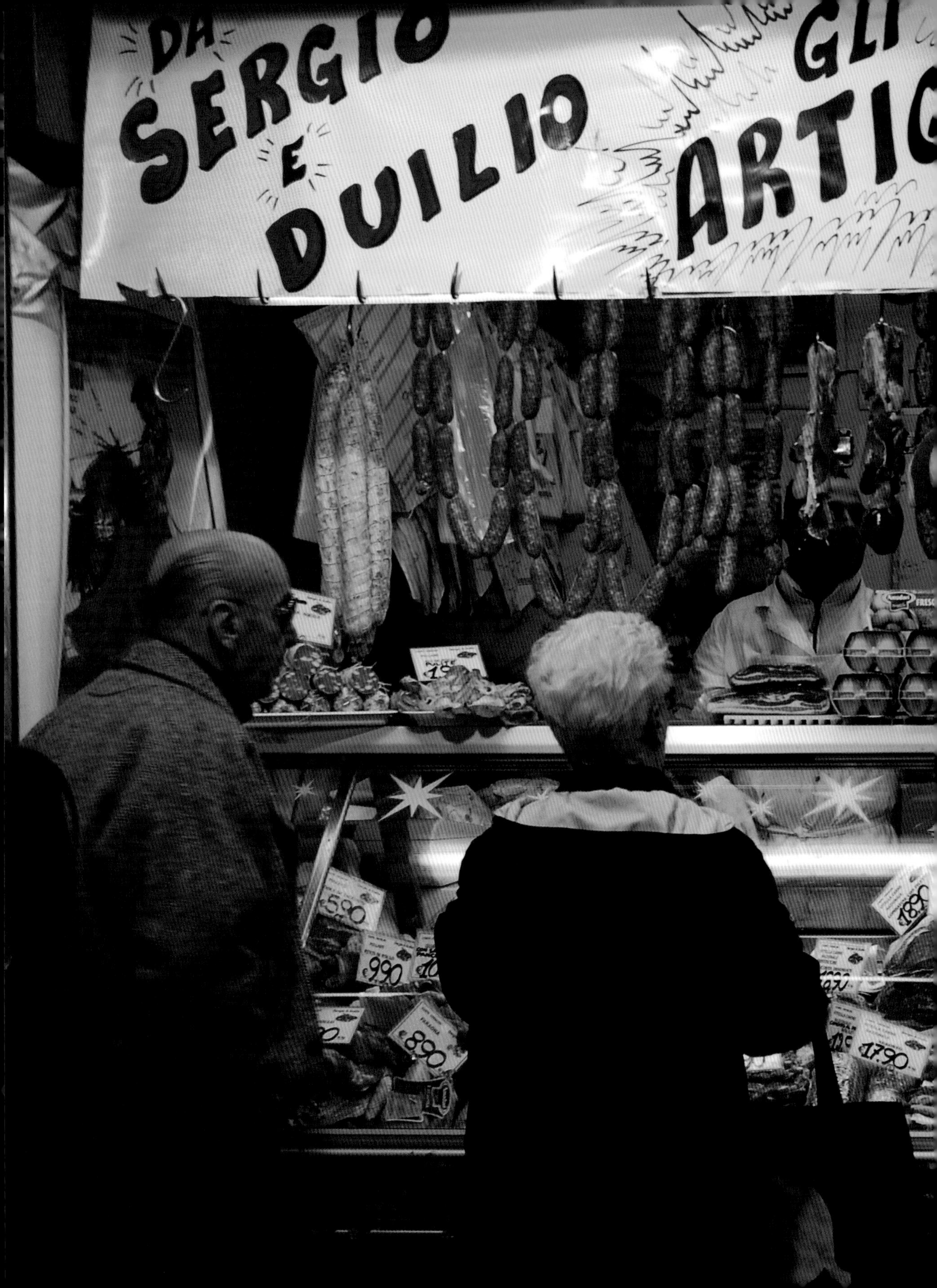
DA
SERGIO
E
DUILIO
GLI
ARTIG
5,90
9,90
8,90
17,90
18,90

ANI
DELLE
NAZIONALI
€8.90
10.90
€5.90
€6.90
13.90
11.90
€7.90
21.90
€5.90
9.90
9.90
€9.90

UOVA IN PURGATORIO CON SCAMORZA
Eggs in Purgatory with Scamorza

If I were stuck in purgatory, I don't think I would mind it as much if I had any dish with tomato sauce and scamorza cheese and some bread *per fare la scarpetta*, to mop up the sauce.

Tomato sauce, eggs, salt, scamorza cheese, fresh basil, extra-virgin olive oil (optional, for drizzling)

This is devilishly easy. It's one of the first things I mastered when I was a kid. I'd take my mother's tomato sauce, pour it into a large pan and heat it up. When it started to bubble, I would crack in a couple of eggs, some salt, and throw in whatever cheese we had in the fridge. Being in an Italian household, it was either Parmigiano, mozzarella, percorino or (now my favorite) scamorza, which I would either slice up or grate into the pan. And all of them work well. I would turn off the heat, tear up some basil and throw that in, then put a lid over the pan and let the eggs poach in the heat of the tomato sauce. While it was cooking, I'd grab a plate and some bread for scooping up the melted smoky scamorza and tomato sauce. Within five minutes, I was having what is still one of my favorite anytime meals.

THE SUNDAY PRANZO

Sunday in the Rocco home, as in Italian homes all around the world, was given over to the tradition of the *pranzo*. A grand meal, usually the grandest of the entire week, it was the time for reconnecting with family—and not just my immediate family, but the extended family of aunts, uncles, cousins, grandparents, even some neighbors and friends, who were invited to sit around the table, eat and visit.

On Sundays, the alchemy that came out of the kitchen wasn't just about the food or the meal, but about how food brought us all together. My mom would say the family that eats together sticks together, and I think there's something to that. And because we got into that routine as kids, now that we're adults we maintain the tradition for ourselves and our children.

At our house, there were rules about the *pranzo*. No television. It was a time to sit together, share stories and catch up on the week. It was a place to connect with the generations. Grandkids would climb up on a grandparent's lap and dunk a little bit of taralli or ciambelle into wine or have their own little glass of wine watered down with a soft drink. The *pranzo* was a rite of passage. The wine was a little treat, but also a lesson for us kids about respecting alcohol.

There was never a children's table where the kids were served a lesser meal than the adults. In fact, I remember as a child being invited to a friend's celebration and being seated at a separate table and fed differently than the adults. Even in grade school, I felt insulted and slighted! The adults got steak, and the kids got hot dogs!

Sunday meals were never very fancy by restaurant standards, just good basic food. My mom loved preparing the *pranzo* because it gave her tremendous pleasure to see this group of people digging into her food. My dad loved sharing his homemade wine, and I loved the way the house smelled and how it filled up with friends and family for those few hours.

Now, don't get me wrong. I like going out to restaurants, but you can't get all that in a restaurant. That's the power of the Sunday *pranzo*, and something you can experience in your own life, even if you don't have family. A communal table, a meal—even a humble one—some wine and a group of friends. That's *dolce vita*, and you can create it yourself, all out of your own kitchen.

STRACOTTO AL CHIANTI
Beef Braised in Chianti

You will not believe how simple and amazing this is. Whenever I serve this stracotto, the next day the phone rings and I'm asked for the recipe. Funny thing is that most people have trouble believing me when I tell them how to make it. They think I'm holding back. I promise that this is all there is to it, and the results will knock your socks off.

Stracotto means "overcooked." There are no real rules about how to cook stracotto al Chianti. I mean, my mother believes you have to sear the meat first, but my grandmother says no, no, no, first the onions. My aunt says the garlic. So as not to offend any of them, I put all three ingredients into the pot at the same time. For me, it's just a simple one-pot meal that you can't screw up. What's fabulous about this recipe is that you can use a less expensive cut of beef because it's going to get cooked for a long, long, long time. The beef will become nice and tender, moist and *molto* succulent.

PER 4 PERSONE

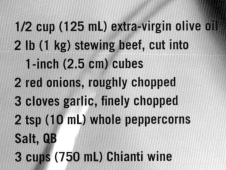

1/2 cup (125 mL) extra-virgin olive oil
2 lb (1 kg) stewing beef, cut into
    1-inch (2.5 cm) cubes
2 red onions, roughly chopped
3 cloves garlic, finely chopped
2 tsp (10 mL) whole peppercorns
Salt, QB
3 cups (750 mL) Chianti wine

Get out your big pot and heat up the olive oil. Once the oil is hot, add the beef, onions and garlic and cook for 2 minutes, stirring frequently. Season with some whole peppercorns and salt, then pour in the wine. The only rule is that you have to have enough wine to completely cover the beef. Bring the wine to a boil, then lower the heat to medium, cover and let the whole thing simmer for approximately 2 hours, stirring it every so often, *e basta!* The result? Perfectly cooked, gorgeously flavored, fork-tender meat. The wine will cook down to give this dish a full-bodied, sweet sauce.

This works really well with polenta or mashed potatoes. Spoon your stracotto right over them for a beautiful presentation, and you have the perfect dead-of-winter meal.

Sometimes in life you just have to treat yourself

I believe you can find *dolce vita* every day just by learning to appreciate the beauty of simplicity. But life needs balance. *Dolce vita* isn't all about creating alchemy with stale bread! There are moments in life when you should absolutely, 100 per cent, step it way up and do something really special. Maybe for you that's a great wine or a bottle of extraordinary olive oil. Or a bottle of balsamic vinegar, aged for more than 25 years so its consistency is syrupy and thick, and the flavor so concentrated that it's more like port than vinegar. Drizzle it over vegetables or a great roast. Maybe it's buying a truffle and enjoying a few shavings over fried eggs.

These are moments that you're sharing with yourself. And that you'll have as a great memory until the next time you treat yourself to something a little bit out of the ordinary.

BACCALÁ ALLA PIZZAIOLA
Codfish in Tomato Oregano Sauce

Baccalá, or salted cod, is one of my favorite fish, and it can be prepared in so many different ways. It can be baked in the oven with potatoes, or braised in white wine or even milk. It also works served cold in a salad. My favorite way to make it, though, is with the classic tomato oregano sauce known as salsa pizzaiola. As a kid, I remember seeing cardboard boxes on the floor at the *mercato,* filled with what looked like dried-out shoe leather. It took me a while to figure out that the moist, flaky fish I loved so much was that "shoe leather."

Baccalá is dried and salted, so you have to buy it well before you want to prepare it. It generally takes a few days to reconstitute, but that's simple. Put it in a bowl and cover it with cold water. Let it stand for two or three days, changing the water three or four times a day. That's important because you want to remove as much of the salt as possible. What you'll end up with is a beautiful white, fleshy meat. Some vendors sell it already reconstituted, but you'll pay a little more.   PER 4 PERSONE

2 lb (1 kg) rehydrated baccalá (salted cod), deboned
All-purpose flour, for dredging
1 1/4 cups (300 mL) extra-virgin olive oil
Salt, QB
Freshly squeezed lemon juice, QB (optional)

For the pizzaiola sauce:
4 tbsp (60 mL) extra-virgin olive oil
2 cloves garlic, chopped
1 can (8 oz/227 mL) crushed tomatoes
1/4 cup (50 mL) capers, drained
1 tbsp (15 mL) chopped fresh oregano
1 chili pepper, crushed (optional)
Salt, QB
1 small bunch fresh flat-leaf parsley,
   finely chopped

Take your rehydrated baccalá out of the water and pat it dry. Cut it into 2-inch (5 cm) slices, sprinkle some flour over them and shake off the excess. You don't want the fish to be too heavy. Heat some olive oil in a pan and fry the baccalá until nice and crisp on all sides. Transfer it to a plate lined with paper towels to drain. At this point, you can enjoy it as is with some salt and a squeeze of lemon.

To make the pizzaiola sauce: Pour the olive oil into a pan. Add the garlic, tomatoes, capers, oregano and chili pepper. For this sauce, you don't want to brown your garlic but rather cook everything together with the crushed tomatoes. The raw garlic and oregano will give that distinctive pizzaiola flavor. Add a pinch of salt and the parsley, then taste it. Remember that baccalá can be salty, so start with only a pinch of salt and go from there. When the flavor is to your liking, add the baccalá and let it cook in the sauce for about a minute.

COZZE A MODO MIO
Mussels alla My Way

This is how my father makes his mussels. And I really do believe that he created this recipe, because every time I'd ask him where he learned it, he'd shrug and say, "Ah, it's *a modo mio*," or "It's *alla* my way." And in the Rocco house, a lot of dishes were kinda "*alla* my way," made up on the fly. If you're nervous about preparing mussels, chill. Don't be intimidated. It's simple. Most of the time, the mussels you get from the fishmonger have already been cleaned, so you really just have to give them a good rinse. Put them in a colander, run water over them, and you're done. Mussels can have bits of seaweed clinging to them, called beards. Just rip them off. Next, you want to make sure the mussels are fresh—and by fresh I mean still alive. There's a simple way to check. First, make sure all the shells are closed. If any are open, press down on them. If they clamp shut, that's good—you know they're fresh, they're alive. If they don't, they're dead, so throw them away.   PER 4 PERSONE

1/4 cup (50 mL) extra-virgin olive oil

2 cloves garlic, finely chopped

Chili pepper flakes

3 lb (1.5 kg) mussels, rinsed and beards removed

1 cup (250 mL) white wine

1 bunch fresh flat-leaf parsley

1/2 cup (125 mL) red wine vinegar

Salt, QB

There are many versions of steamed mussels: with tomato sauce, diced tomatoes, cherry tomatoes and even *al vino bianco*—with just white wine. But all the versions start off the same way.

Heat your pan over high heat. Put in the olive oil, the garlic and the "Rocco family must"—chili pepper flakes. The joke in our family is that we love chili peppers so much we even put them on our cereal.

When the garlic is slightly browned, throw in your mussels. Put the lid on the pan to steam the mussels, giving the pan a little shake. After 30 to 60 seconds, pour in the wine. It may seem that a cup of wine isn't much for a recipe that feeds four, but the mussels actually release a lot of liquid as they steam, mixing with the wine to create a flavorful broth. Put the lid back on and give the pan a shake every so often.

While the mussels are steaming, chop some flat-leaf parsley. Now, my dad calls this "*alla* my way" because he adds a little bit of red wine vinegar. So when you've finished chopping the parsley, lift the lid and add the parsley, red wine vinegar and a little bit of salt. Put the lid back on, give the pan a shake and let it cook some more. Don't be afraid to remove the lid, grab a spoon and taste the broth. You may want to add more salt, more chili pepper flakes or maybe even a bit more red wine vinegar for that extra hit of contrast. If you want to pour in a bit more wine, that's okay, because the alcohol will burn off, and the wine will lend a nice sweetness to your broth. It should take barely 5 minutes for this dish to be done. You know it's ready when all the shells have opened. If any of shells haven't opened, discard them—they're not good.

Polpo

A lot of people get really freaked out at the idea of eating octopus, never mind handling it raw. Okay, I have to admit it can look gross and a bit creepy if you're not used to it. But it's wonderfully tender and succulent, and well worth the minimal effort. This is another one-pot meal that's so easy—let me tell you a story about just how easy.

When my niece Madeleine was five, she was hanging out at our place on Christmas Eve. We decided we would bring polpo in umido to our family's big Christmas dinner that evening. Madeleine wanted to spend time with her "favorite uncle," so she came into the kitchen with me. I got her standing on a chair and, with my supervision, she prepared the whole dish, from cleaning to cooking. We had a blast. At dinner that night, she ate the octopus with us, partly out of pride because she'd prepared it and partly because she saw the rest of us enjoying it.

I tell you that story for two reasons: one, this dish is so easy a five-year-old can do it, so you can, too; two, if you get your kids involved, they'll develop not only a love for the kitchen and confidence, but also a sense of adventure and appreciation for food that they'll take with them for the rest of their lives.

Unless you live by the sea, it's likely going to be tough to find a fresh octopus. You're probably going to be buying a frozen or thawed-from-frozen octopus, and that's okay.

POLPO IN UMIDO
Stewed Octopus

2 lb (1 kg) octopus, cut into 1-inch (2.5 cm) cubes
4 tbsp (60 mL) extra-virgin olive oil
3 cloves garlic, finely chopped
Chili peppers, crushed, QB (optional)
5 anchovies
20 capers, drained
12 cherry tomatoes, quartered
1 bunch fresh flat-leaf parsley
Salt, QB

So the first thing I'll teach you is how to clean the octopus. You need to remove the beak, which is smack in the middle, between the tentacles. With your paring knife, scoop out the dark, hard shell. Now put the octopus under cold running water and give it a really good rinse; make sure you clean the inside of the sac to get out all the sandy grit. If you want, you can just cut it off and clean it separately, or discard it altogether. Personally, I keep it intact and rinse it well. Once it's clean, cut the octopus into little cubes, about 1 inch (2.5 cm).

Now that the hard work is done, get out your pot, heat up the olive oil and add the garlic, chili peppers, if you wish, anchovies and capers. Stir for a few minutes or so to help dissolve a little of the anchovies and to let the garlic brown. At this point, add your cut octopus and cherry tomatoes and stir so everything is well mixed. The cool thing about this recipe is that it doesn't call for any wine, vegetable stock or fish stock. The octopus releases so much liquid that it flavors the dish. Make sure your heat is on medium and throw in the parsley and a little salt. There are a lot of salty ingredients in this recipe—anchovies, capers and the octopus itself, which retains a lot of sea water—so go easy with the salt. You can always add more later.

Put a lid on the pot and let it cook on medium for about 1 1/2 hours, giving it a stir every so often, until the octopus is delicate and fork-tender. Serve warm or at room temperature. The tomatoes cook down and create a thick sauce that gives the final dish the texture of a stew, with loads of flavor.

PER 4 PERSONE

Un' altra idea: Make extra because this tastes great the next day. Better yet, throw some of the leftovers on top of spaghetti along with a good drizzle of olive oil and you have pasta al polpo.

Dolci

This section is a little tricky for me, and especially counterintuitive to the message of this book. I'm not a big dessert maker. To make pastries, you really need to pay attention to precise measurements. No self-respecting pastry chef would be throwing around the philosophy of *quanto basta!*

To be honest, pastry making isn't part of daily life in most Italian kitchens. Which doesn't mean there aren't killer Italian baked desserts, but Italians tend to head out to the *pasticceria* and enjoy their fancy desserts in a café with an espresso. Or they buy a torta to take to a friend's home for dessert.

But you can't have the *dolce vita* without the dolce, so I've come up with a selection of dessert recipes that will satisfy the need for an end-of-the-meal sweet and are, for the most part, *quanto basta.*

TIRAMISÙ AL LIMONE
Lemon Tiramisù

Traditional tiramisù is probably one of Italy's most famous exports, right up there with Sophia Loren, the Vespa and Nutella. It's usually made by dipping the cookies into coffee. I was inspired to make this variation after spending time in Ravello, a gorgeous town on the Amalfi coast in southern Italy that's famous for its lemons and its limoncello liqueur. This is surprisingly fast and easy, and there's no baking involved. **PER 8–10 PERSONE**

4 egg yolks
1/2 cup (125 mL) sugar, plus extra if desired
Juice of half a lemon
2 cups (500 mL) mascarpone
Zest of 1 lemon, plus extra for sprinkling
2 cups (500 mL) whipping cream (35%)
1 cup (250 mL) limoncello, plus an extra splash
1/3 to 1/2 cup (75 to 125 mL) water
40 Italian savoiardi (ladyfingers)
White chocolate, shaved, for topping (or lemon zest)

Whisk together the egg yolks, 4 tbsp (60 mL) of the sugar and the lemon juice until uniform. Add the mascarpone and lemon zest and keep whisking until they are well incorporated. Taste it. At this point, it's so delicious you'll have to restrain yourself from eating the whole bowl! But it only gets better.

In another bowl, combine the whipping cream, remaining sugar and a splash of the limoncello and whip it until stiff peaks form. Add it to the mascarpone mixture, gently folding it together.

At this point, in a traditional tiramisù, you'd pour coffee into a bowl and dip the cookies in it. But since we're using limoncello, you may want to go a bit easy. So pour the rest of the limoncello into a bowl. I recommend adding a splash of water, 1/3 to a 1/2 cup (75 to 125 mL), depending on your taste.

One at a time, dip—don't soak—both sides of the ladyfingers in the limoncello mixture. The exterior should be wet, but the interior should remain dry. As you finish dipping each ladyfinger, put it in the bottom of a cake pan. Pack them in tightly. Once you've completed that layer, spread half of the cream mixture evenly over the cookies, making sure they're completely covered. Then make a second layer of dipped ladyfingers and evenly spread the remaining cream mixture on top. Sprinkle the tiramisù with lemon zest and white chocolate. Ideally, let it rest in the fridge for a few hours to let the flavors settle. But in a pinch, you can serve it immediately.

BRUTTI MA BUONI
Ugly but Good

These cookies aren't really ugly, but they're definitely good and easy to make. The name comes from the fact that they don't have a regular cookie shape. These are native to Tuscany and were invented to use up egg whites, because so many Tuscan dishes call for the yolk. This is a very forgiving cookie recipe in that a little extra of an ingredient won't sabotage it.   **MAKES 24 COOKIES**

6 egg whites
1 cup (250 mL) toasted almonds, coarsely chopped
1 cup (250 mL) toasted hazelnuts, coarsely chopped
3/4 cup (175 mL) sugar
1 tbsp (15 mL) all-purpose flour, plus extra for dusting
1 tbsp (15 mL) cocoa powder
1 tbsp (15 mL) amaretto
1 1/2 tsp (7 mL) vanilla extract
Butter, for greasing cookie sheet

Put the egg whites in a bowl and beat them until they get very airy and form nice white peaks. It's important that the peaks not break, so don't overbeat them. The airiness gives the cookie its light texture, so don't dump in your other ingredients. Instead, sprinkle in the almonds, hazelnuts, sugar, flour, cocoa powder, amaretto and vanilla. Now gently, gently fold everything together.

Grease a cookie tray with some butter, dust it with a little flour and then use a spoon to drop the dough onto the tray in little blobs, leaving approximately 1 inch (2.5 cm) between each one. Bake for 20 to 30 minutes or until golden and firm to the touch. If you like chewier cookies, underbake them slightly. Remove them from the oven and transfer them to a wire rack. Let them rest for 30 minutes or until cooled.

CIAMBELLE
Semi-Hard Doughnuts

Don't let the thought of making doughnuts overwhelm you. These are more like biscotti than traditional doughnuts. They're also healthier because they're baked, not fried. And they're not as sweet as the typical doughnut. In fact, the custom is to dip them in wine as an after-dinner treat. They also work well dunked in milk or coffee for breakfast.

The measurements are a no-brainer, because aside from the flour and aniseeds, there are equal parts of all the other ingredients. You might be surprised to find aniseeds in the ingredient list. They add an interesting, mildly licorice flavor to the ciambelle, and a little goes a long way.

MAKES ABOUT 24 DOUGHNUTS

4 to 5 cups (1 to 1.25 L) all-purpose flour
1 cup (250 mL) sugar
1 cup (250 mL) extra-virgin olive oil
1 cup (250 mL) white wine
2 tbsp (30 mL) aniseeds

The first thing you might have noticed in the ingredient list is the range given for the flour. The actual amount you'll end up using will depend on the kind of flour you have, which will depend on the brand. As well, the humidity in the air is going to affect the way this comes together, so you should go by feel.

Pour 4 cups (1 L) of the flour onto a big work surface and create a well in the middle. To the well, add the sugar, olive oil, wine and aniseeds.

Now with your hands, slowly start to incorporate everything. If you need to add more flour, sprinkle it in a bit at a time. Knead until it becomes an even dough. You'll end up with a dense cookie dough.

To make the ciambelle: Cut off a piece of the dough and roll it into a log. Cut the log into strips. Form a doughnut-like shape by pinching together the opposite ends of each strip to form a little circle. Continue until all the dough has been used up. Put the ciambelle on a cookie sheet covered with parchment paper and then into a 400° to 450°F (200° to 230°C) oven for 12 to 15 minutes or until golden. Let them cool, then enjoy!

Panna cotta is a traditional Italian dessert that literally translates as the very unromantic and unappetizing sounding "cooked cream." It's delicious and impressive looking, and much easier to make than most people think. There are a lot of variations, using different fruits or even chocolate. But here I give you a basic recipe, with a mixed berry sauce. Once you've mastered the basic technique, pick your favorite fruit and make the dish your own.

I learned to make this dessert from a friend's mother, a fantastic cook who, like most Italian cooks, practises *quanto basta.* She said to me, "*Non ci sono misure*—there are no real measurements. Just a little cream, maybe a little milk, some sugar and honey." I'm giving you measurements here, but this dessert isn't overly picky when it comes to exact quantities. It's very forgiving. Some recipes call only for cream, but I find it too heavy, so I add milk—about a third of the quantity of cream. Once you've made it a few times, you'll decide what works for you.   **PER 4-6 PERSONE**

1 1/2 cups (375 mL) whipping cream (35%)
1/2 cup (125 mL) milk
1/4 cup (50 mL) sugar
1 tbsp (15 mL) liquid honey
3 sheets unflavored gelatin

For the mixed berry sauce:
2 cups (500 mL) water
2 cups (500 mL) mixed fresh berries
2 tbsp (30 mL) sugar

Pour the cream and milk into a pan over medium heat and stir in the sugar and honey until all the ingredients melt together. Add the gelatin and continue stirring until they're fully dissolved. Just before the cream and milk come to a boil, remove the pan from the heat. Pour the mixture through a strainer to remove the foam. This ensures that the panna cotta has that famous velvety consistency.

Pour into little bowls, ramekins or, for a fancier presentation, wine or martini glasses. Let cool for half an hour or so, then put them in the fridge for a few hours to solidify.

To top the panna cotta: You can use any fresh berries you like. Just sprinkle them with a little bit of sugar, a splash of your favorite liqueur, like grappa, Grand Marnier or brandy, and let sit for 15 or 20 minutes before serving. Or you can make a mixed berry sauce: In a pot, combine the water, berries and sugar and bring to a boil. Lower the heat and simmer for 15 to 20 minutes or until the sauce is reduced by half and thickened up. Serve it either warm or cold over your panna cotta.

To serve: If you used ramekins, loosen each panna cotta by running a knife blade around the inside edge of the ramekin. Then flip it onto your serving plate and tap the bottom gently to unmould. Pour the topping over each and serve. If you used a wine or martini glass, just pour the sauce or fresh berries over top and serve. It's heaven in a glass. Definitely don't worry if you

CROCCANTE DI MANDORLE
Almond Brittle

This recipe makes me think of Christmas. My mom and my aunts used to go into production mode on this treat before the holidays. I recommend having the ingredients on hand. It comes together so fast and is universally loved. It's also a perfect example of alchemy—how just two ingredients, almonds and sugar, are transformed into an incredible treat.

This is as easy as it gets. It's really about paying attention and working quickly. It's incredibly forgiving and can be eyeballed. The key is making sure the sugar doesn't burn but turns to a deep golden brown.

MAKES A GOOD BATCH

3 cups (750 mL) sugar
Up to 1/2 cup (125 mL) water (optional)
4 cups (1 L) whole almonds

Heat up your pot over high heat and add the sugar. Keep stirring. You'll see that it begins to sweat and liquefy. Add a bit of water if you think it needs help. Keep going, cooking and stirring until the sugar is completely liquefied and turns a rich deep brown. Now in go the almonds. Mix really well to make sure they're fully coated. Cook it all together in the pot for a few minutes, stirring constantly so it doesn't stick, until the almonds are toasted. Remove the pot from the heat and, working quickly, pour the hot almond mixture onto a cookie sheet to the desired thickness. Let it cool. If you can stand it, wait about half an hour, then break it up into smaller pieces. Now you can eat it.

GELATO AFFOGATO
Drowned Ice Cream

The beauty of this dessert is that it's so incredibly simple, yet it's a perfect way to finish a meal, even if you're not an espresso drinker. You'll find the combination of these two ingredients amazingly delicate. This is another example of what you can do with a few good basics. I always have good vanilla ice cream on hand. And, of course, I have my espresso maker. So if company comes by unexpectedly, I have dessert.

For each serving, place 2 scoops of vanilla ice cream in a glass. Pour hot espresso over the ice cream and serve immediately, before the ice cream melts.

PARMIGIANO CON NOCI E MIELE
Parmigiano with Honey and Walnuts

This, to me, is the essence of *dolce vita*. I've put it in the Dolci section because it's a great way to finish a meal, but it could just as easily be served as a snack any time of the day or night. And it's a low-stress way of entertaining.

The centerpiece is a hunk of fantastic Parmigiano-Reggiano and some honey to drizzle over it. To make it even better, lay out a selection of nuts and dried fruits—walnuts, pine nuts, pears, grapes, dried figs, apricots. Serve with port or red wine. **PER 4 PERSONE**

14 oz (400 g) Parmigiano-Reggiano cheese
4 tbsp (60 mL) liquid honey
1 cup (250 mL) walnuts, halved
Dried figs (optional)
Pine nuts (optional)

FRAGOLE ALL' ACETO BALSAMICO
Strawberries with Balsamic Vinegar

For this recipe, look for real *aceto balsamico*. The authentic stuff comes from Modena, Italy, and is aged like wine. As it gets older, the texture becomes thick and syrupy, and the flavor concentrates and is luxurious. The younger balsamics are good for salad dressings, but for desserts like this one, I recommend splurging a bit on a bottle that's aged at least twelve years. A little goes a long way. And trust me, you'll find other uses for it as well.

The blend of balsamic vinegar, the pepper and the strawberries creates an explosion of flavors. And, of course, you can vary the quantities to suit your taste. These measurements are based on a serving of a cup (250 mL) of strawberries per person. But if you love strawberries, double it!

PER 4 PERSONE

4 cups (1 L) strawberries, hulled and quartered
2 tbsp (30 mL) sugar
5 tbsp (75 mL) balsamic vinegar
Freshly ground pepper, QB

Quarter your strawberries. Sprinkle them with the sugar and drizzle with the balsamic vinegar. I like to add a few grinds of pepper, which gives an interesting little kick. Let it sit for 5 minutes, then serve.

Un' altra idea: Drizzle that great balsamic you've just bought over premium vanilla ice cream. You'll be blown away by how good it tastes.

ZABAGLIONE CON PANNA MONTATA
Zabaglione with Whipped Cream

Every day before we went to school, my mom would make us a semi-shot of Marsala wine beaten up with a raw egg yolk and some sugar so that, as she said, our bones would grow stronger.

As an eight-year-old, I didn't think, "Ah, the classic ingredients of a zabaglione." I just wanted to get Flintstones Chewables like the rest of my pals. But my mom, the same mom who banned soft drinks, believed, as her mom had, that it was perfectly normal to start a child's day off that way. And now, as an adult, those flavors are etched in my mind. Every time I have this classic Italian dessert, I chuckle and think of our morning ritual.

Zabaglione is usually made with Marsala, but I've also made it with Vin Santo, the classic Tuscan dessert wine. It has a velvety texture that goes wonderfully over fruit or ice cream, or it can be eaten on its own. I've added my own spin on the tradition by including whipped cream.   **PER 4 PERSONE**

6 large egg yolks
6 tbsp (90 mL) sugar
6 tbsp (90 mL) Marsala or Vin Santo wine
1 cup (250 mL) whipping cream (35%)
1/2 cup (125 mL) fresh blueberries

When making zabaglione, the rule of thumb per serving is 1 or 2 egg yolks, depending on the size of the eggs, 1 tbsp (15 mL) sugar, and 1 tbsp (15 mL) Marsala or Vin Santo.

Put a pot filled with water on the stove and bring it to a boil. At that point, lower it to a gentle boil.

Next, in a stainless-steel bowl, whisk together the egg yolks, sugar and Marsala until blended. Hold the bowl over the pot of boiling water, whisking constantly. You can let the bowl touch the water slightly, but don't let it rest there for too long. This is a bit of a dance because you don't want the eggs to overcook or you'll end up with scrambled eggs. You want the yolk mixture to become light and creamy, so you might have to lift the bowl from time to time, but keep whisking. You'll get the idea as you go. If you need to lower the heat, do so, but keep whisking until you reach that thick, silky and creamy consistency, which takes between 3 and 5 minutes.

In a separate bowl, whip the cream until it forms soft peaks. Gently fold the yolk mixture into the whipped cream with a rubber spatula. When it's combined, refrigerate it for about 30 minutes or until you're ready for it. Serve in glasses with blueberries on top.

MELANZANE AL CIOCCOLATO
Chocolate Eggplant

The first time I had this combination was at my friend Eddie Oliva's family's restaurant, Il Pinguino, in the small town of Scala, on the Amalfi coast. For dinner, we had pasta with eggplant and pizza with eggplant. Then for dessert, the waiter brought us a cake made out of layers of eggplant and chocolate.

Now, Eddie and his brothers are famous practical jokers, and they know I love eggplant, so I wasn't sure whether they had made up this crazy dessert to get a reaction. And then I took a bite. The combination of the bittersweet dark chocolate and the neutral, meaty eggplant was mind blowing. It turns out that chocolate eggplant is no joke, but has been enjoyed for years in Amalfi and Sicily. When I came home, I made my adaptation. Rather than a layer cake, my version is lighter and more delicate, and is topped with toasted hazelnuts or almonds. It's not something you'll want every night of the week, but once you've tried it, it's a treat you'll crave every so often. **PER 4 PERSONE**

2 eggplants, thinly sliced
Coarse sea salt
Extra-virgin olive oil, for frying
All-purpose flour, for dredging
1 lb (500 g) bittersweet chocolate, cut into small pieces
1 cup (250 mL) milk
1 cup (250 mL) toasted hazelnuts or almonds, chopped

Prepare the eggplant by salting the slices and laying them in a colander for 30 minutes to sweat out any bitterness. Rinse under cold water and blot dry.

In a deep-sided frying pan, heat the olive oil until very hot.

Dredge the eggplant slices in flour and gently add them, a few at a time, to the hot oil. Don't overcrowd the pan or the temperature of the oil will drop and the eggplant won't crisp up. Fry the eggplant on both sides until golden, which should only take a few minutes. Place them on a plate covered with paper towels to absorb the excess oil.

Now for the chocolate. Put a pot of water on the stove and bring it to a boil. Place the chocolate pieces in a stainless steel mixing bowl and rest it over the pot of boiling water. As the chocolate melts, whisk in the milk until the chocolate becomes liquid and velvety.

Arrange your eggplant slices on a serving dish. Drizzle them with melted chocolate and sprinkle the toasted nuts on top. Let come to room temperature before serving.

Cin Cin

A bottle of wine is a classic on any Italian table. But sometimes you need a drink that's a little fancier, and that's where the cocktail comes in. Italian cocktails express sophistication and seasonality. With that in mind, here are a few very simple ones that anyone can whip up, for those occasions when you want to treat yourself.

LIMONCELLO DI VILLA MARIA
Villa Maria's Limoncello

This is the quintessential drink of the Amalfi coast, where the flavorful lemons are kissed by the Mediterranean sun and grow in almost every backyard. It seems that most families have their own version. This was given to me by my buddy Il Professore, who makes it every week for his hotel Villa Maria in Ravello. Once you've made it a couple of times, you can adapt it to be as strong or as sweet as you like. **MAKES APPROXIMATELY 7 CUPS (1.75 L)**

Rind of 7 ripe organic lemons, washed and dried
4 cups (1 L) 95% alcohol
4 cups (1 L) boiling water
1 lb (500 g) sugar

For this recipe, you'll need a large glass bottle or jar with a capacity of approximately 16 cups (4 L).

Shave off the yellow part of the lemon rind using a potato peeler. Put the rinds in the large glass bottle and pour in the pure alcohol. Cover the bottle with plastic wrap; make sure it's really well sealed or the alcohol will evaporate and you'll be left with a jar of peels. Allow these lucky lemon peels to bathe in the alcohol at room temperature for 12 days. This is in part why it's important to use the best-quality lemons you can find—the peels are what give you the lemon color and flavor.

After 12 days, get back to the kitchen. Boil some water, enough so that you have 4 cups (1 L). Add the sugar and stir until it has all dissolved. Let it cool. Remove the lemon rinds from the alcohol and add the sugared water. Reseal your glass bottle tightly to prevent evaporation, and let that sit for another 10 days. After 10 days, you have limoncello. It's best served chilled as a digestive after a meal.

ASTI SPUMANTE CON CILANTRO
Asti Spumante with Cilantro

Asti Spumante is a sweet sparkling wine, generally served as a cocktail or with dessert. This is a cocktail that I serve in the summer. The cilantro is a surprising addition to this bubbly, but it adds a herby, citrus-like summertime flavor. The most important thing is that the Asti Spumante be chilled.

1 bunch cilantro, tied
1 lime, halved
1 bottle (750 mL) Asti Spumante, chilled

Tie your cilantro into a neat bunch, drop it into a large jug and "bruise it" by crushing it with a wooden spoon to help release the flavor. Next, squeeze in the lime juice and drop in the lime halves. Pour in your chilled Asti Spumante, give it a good stir and serve.

NEGRONI

This is a classic Italian aperitivo. The formula is equal parts of all three ingredients.

Sweet vermouth (Martini & Rossi), gin, Campari

Or try the Milanese variation, called Negroni Sbagliato, which translates roughly as "a Negroni with a mistake in it."

Sweet vermouth, prosecco, Campari

Not a bad mistake!

PESCHE CON VINO
Drunken Peaches

When I was growing up, this was something we used to have all the time in the late summer, when sweet peaches were abundant.

PER 6 PERSONE

6 peaches
1 bottle (750 mL) Chianti Classico wine
1 tbsp (15 mL) sugar
1 tsp (5 mL) cinnamon

Cut each peach into 8 wedges and put them in a pitcher. Pour in the Chianti, and add the sugar and cinnamon. Refrigerate for half an hour to allow the flavors to marry.

MILLE GRAZIE

To everyone at HarperCollins Canada for believing in this book and for being so excited from the day I walked into their office. Kirsten Hanson, my editor, who honored my vision and style, and worked so hard to make sure it all came together. Alan Jones, for your patience and insight. Julia Armstrong, for your edit and for keeping my voice. And Noelle Zitzer, for your hard work and guidance, and for always being available when I had a question.

Big thanks to Karen Gordon for your passion, talent and skill in capturing my voice with good humor and style. You're a good friend, and you make me laugh!

Francesco Lastrucci, for your brilliant photography. Amazing what can be accomplished in just a few weeks, with a little sleep, good food, wine and friendship! Bernardo Galli, for your hospitality and for allowing me to completely take over your home during the shoot.

Rutendo Sabeta, for your great eye not only in selecting photos but in helping with the look of the book. You're a talent! The Rockhead Entertainment family and crew, for all the support over the years. Joanna McIntyre, for your love, honesty and integrity. You are always there for me! And to Lucas Labrecque, our associate producer, editor and friend. You are sweet like a *babà*!

TLN Telelatino and Aldo DeFelice, for supporting the series and trusting me as much as you have. Greg Cameron and JVC, for your generosity. And Food Network Canada, for taking a chance on us way back when. This book is a result of the TV series!

To all the people in this book—the chefs, cooks, market vendors, Italian friends I met along the way who loved to share recipes and meals—you inspired me to cook and to write this book. You all live in its pages!

My mom, Josie, and dad, Mimmo, for your love, unconditional support and passion for food, family and tradition. My sister, Maria, and brother, Sal; my in-laws, Maria and Peter; my grandparents, aunts, uncles and cousins who are way too many to name—thanks for the family celebrations with good food, wine and conversation.

To my wife, Nina, who believed and never doubted. And to my beautiful daughters, Emma and Giorgia, my joy, who inspire me daily. Love you guys!

INDEX